EXPLORING THE WORLD OF

FOSSILS

EXPLORING

THE WORLD OF

FOS

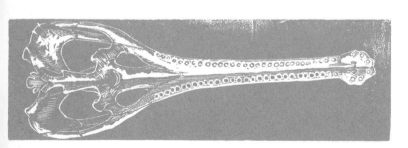

S I L S

by WILLIAM H. MATTHEWS III

artists: Corinne & Robert Borja

CHILDRENS PRESS Chicago

Library of Congress Catalog Card Number: 64-19884
Copyright © 1964, Childrens Press
Published simultaneously in Canada.

Contents

William H. Matthews, Professor of Geology at Lamar State College of Technology, Beaumont, Texas, is the author of many books on earth history at an older level.

STORIES
IN
STONE

Have you ever found a "sea-shell" high in the mountains or far from the ocean? Did you wonder how it came to be left high and dry? And maybe you wondered why it felt a little heavier and looked a little older than the shells that you picked up at the beach last summer.

Well, that land-locked shell was probably a lot older than the shell at the beach—in fact it may have been many *millions* of years older! The geologists, men who know and study rocks, tell us that this shell is a fossil.

What is a fossil?

A fossil is the remains or evidence of a prehistoric plant or animal. It usually represents the hard part of some ancient organism that once lived in the area in which it was found. It might be the tooth of a great shark or the shell of a tiny snail. Or perhaps the backbone of a mighty dinosaur or the imprint of a delicate leaf—all of these are fossils and each has a fascinating story to tell.

Reliefing Dinosaur bones
in the quarry at Dinosaur
National Monument, Utah.
Courtesy of National Park Service

woolly mammoth

Worthenia   trilobite

Many times the fossil hunter must also be a detective. The actual skeleton or hard parts of an animal may have been destroyed, but its tracks and footprints were preserved in the rocks. When studied by the *paleontologist,* an expert on fossils, much can be learned about the animal that made the tracks. Footprints, for example, commonly provide information as to the length and weight of a dinosaur. A certain type of hole in a clam shell will tell us that a hungry meat-eating snail bored its way into the shell and made a meal of the soft parts of the unfortunate clam. We may not find any fossil snails with the clam shell, but the snail left clues which enable the paleo-detective to solve the crime!

Once in a very great while we find a fossil that has actually been preserved in "cold storage" in nature's own deep-freeze. Ancient elephants have been found in Siberia where they were trapped in the ice as long as 25,000 years ago. Yet when the ice melted the bodies of these elephants were found in such good condition that the flesh could be eaten by dogs and the tusks sold by ivory traders!

Most fossils, however, are preserved in stone and must be studied in comparison with living forms.

The type of fossil most commonly collected consists of the remains of *invertebrates*. These are animals that did not have backbones. They may, for example, be fossil snails, clams, corals, or some other spineless animal.

12

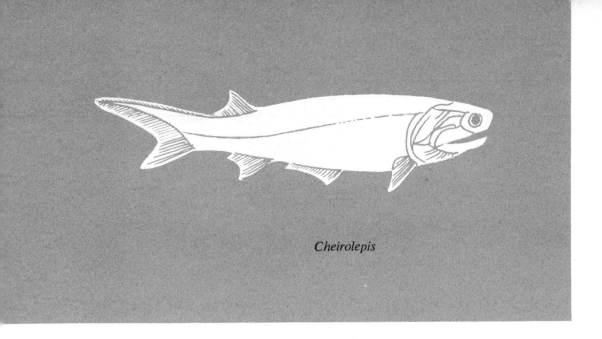

Cheirolepis

These fossils usually represent the shells of animals that lived in prehistoric seas which once covered the area in which they were collected. Some of them are so well preserved that they look much as they did when they lived on the bottom of the sea hundreds of millions of years ago. Many of these fossil shells closely resemble their relatives that are living today. These animals all had their skeletons on the outside of their bodies. Prehistoric animals that did not have any hard parts had little chance of becoming fossilized.

The rocks in which the fossils are found represent sand or mud deposited as sediment on the bottom of the ancient seas in which the animals lived. But they are not always found in good condition. Indeed, since the fossils are many thousands or millions of years old we can hardly expect them to look brand new.

The *vertebrates,* animals with backbones, have their bony hard parts inside their bodies. A paleontologist who studies the skeletons of prehistoric animals with backbones is called a *vertebrate paleontologist.*

The most familiar vertebrate fossils are the dinosaurs, a group of extinct reptiles. These left some large bones, for some dinosaurs were as much as 85 feet long and weighed 50 tons. During the dinosaur age there were all sorts and sizes of strange reptiles. Some swam and looked like fish. Others flew and looked like birds—but that is another story. We will learn more of these interesting creatures later on in this book.

13

It is also possible to find the bones and teeth of fossil horses, camels, and elephants. Some of these are so well preserved that you might mistake them for the remains of recent animals. However, fossil bones usually have some of their hollow spaces filled with minerals and this makes them heavier than recent bones.

Animal remains are not the only kinds of fossils that one might find. Plants are also found as fossils. These usually occur as leaf impressions or parts of trunks or branches of trees. When plants die and their remains become covered with sediment they lose certain gases and liquids and may be turned into carbon. This is the way in which coal is formed. In fact, coal is composed almost entirely of the remains of plants that have been dead for millions of years.

Tree trunks and branches are often *petrified*—literally turned to stone. Over the ages certain trees were buried by sediments and became soaked with underground water. The water that saturated the wood contained minerals which gradually took the place of the woody tissue as it slowly decayed. The mineral that most commonly replaced wood is *quartz*. Quartz is composed of *silica*—a substance that is common in glass and sand. As each cell becomes filled with silica the tree gets heavier and more stonelike until it is completely turned to stone. Many times other minerals are deposited along with the quartz and these form the beautiful colors seen in some petrified wood.

Perhaps you have visited the famous Petrified Forest of Arizona. Here large numbers of petrified logs are scattered about on the ground as if some prehistoric lumberman had gone through the forest with his saw. Some of these fossil trees are so faithfully preserved that you can even see the rings that show the growth of the tree. But you don't have to go to Arizona to find petrified wood—it is found in almost every state.

By now you may be wondering about such queer goings-on as a stone forest on an Arizona desert, and fossil sea-shells in the mountains. For hundreds of years many people wondered about such odd happenings. The only explanations that they could offer were based on fear and superstition. Then with the birth of the science of geology the pieces of this gigantic jig-saw puzzle slowly began to fit into place—we could finally read these stories in stone.

For example, we now know that the land surrounding the Petrified Forest has not always been as we see it today. Millions of years ago this area was probably a low, flat, river plain. Some of the streams flowing across these flat lands brought in large numbers of logs from neighboring mountainous areas. These dead trees accumulated into large log-jams, became waterlogged, and slowly settled to the bottom. While they lay on the river bottom the logs gradually became covered with river mud and the ashes produced by nearby volcanoes. Slowly, year after year, the processes of petrifaction did their work. Finally, millions of years later, great upheavals within the earth

The Petrified Forest of Arizona
probably looked much like this
millions of years ago.

*Movements of the earth
and the seas gradually uncovered
the fossils we find today.*

raised the land to its present level and the fossil trees were uncovered by the process of erosion.

The geologist has also learned that the lands and the seas have not always occupied the same positions that they have today. During certain times in the early history of the earth the seas have been in areas where there are now plains and mountains. Throughout the ages the seas have moved back and forth across much of the continent bringing with them the sea life of the time, and leaving behind sediments in the form of sand, mud, and shells.

As vast thicknesses of mud and sand accumulated, the sediments on the bottom became tightly packed and very hard—they were beginning to turn into rocks. Some of these rocks contain the shells, teeth, and bones of animals that had lived in the ancient seas.

Much later our earth had "growing pains"—volcanoes, earthquakes, and other great disturbances. Earth movements associated with these disturbances raised the fossil-bearing rocks high above sea level where they are found today. Here they were exposed to the action of the wind and rain which eventually washed the fossils from their surrounding rocks.

The rocky layers of the earth's crust are like the pages of a book, and fossils are like pictures in stone. True, there are many pages missing from this book for the entire story is not known with certainty. There is, however, enough information to provide us with an interesting account of the many unusual and fascinating animals of long ago, and of the world in which they lived.

Turn back to the earliest pages of our rocky "book" of earth history? Would you like to know more about the early plants and animals that lived on this earth of ours? You will find it to be a most interesting story that began more than three billion years ago.

16

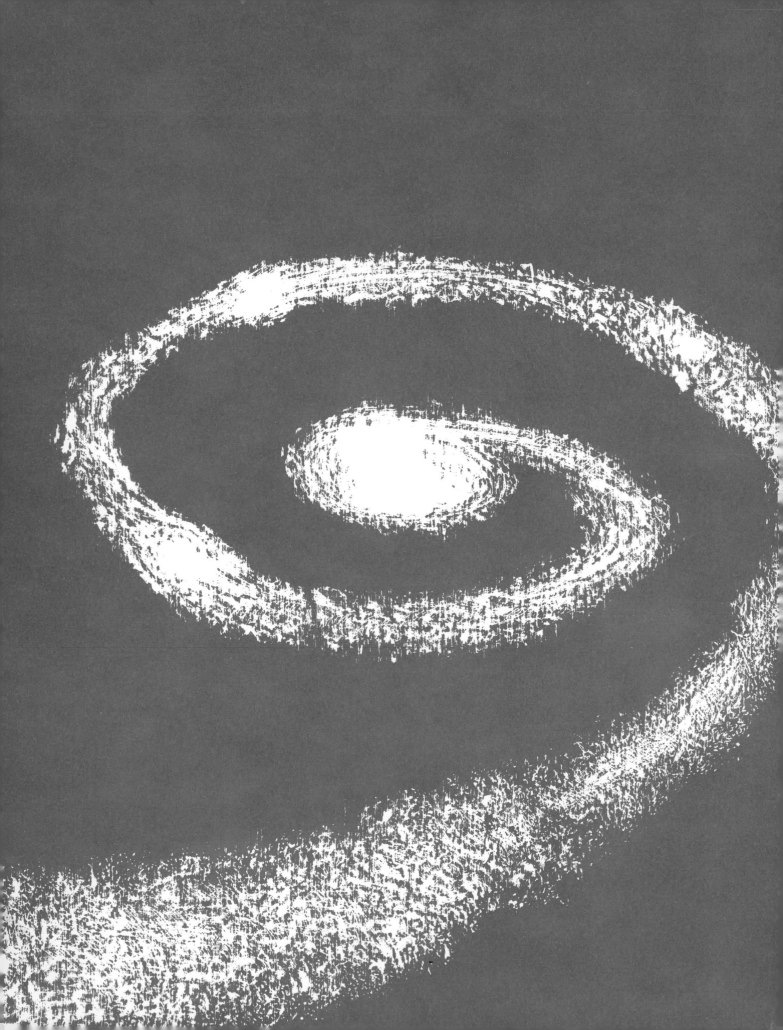

THE EARTH'S BEGINNINGS

Where did our earth come from? How and when was it formed? These are questions that have perplexed man since the dawn of history. At first, primitive people tried to find answers to these questions in myths and superstition. But in the last hundred years more scientific means have been used in an attempt to determine the age and origin of our planet. Yet despite the great amount of work that has been done on these problems, they still cannot be answered with certainty. Scientists have, however, come up with some "educated guesses" that have shed considerable light on these questions.

Although a variety of theories have been proposed to explain the origin of the earth, the latest of these all seem to agree on one basic fact. The sun is the parent body of the nine planets in our solar system. Thus, according to one theory, the sun and other members of the solar system were originally a cloud of gas and dust swirling through outer space. These particles gradually shrank and became consolidated to form a great spinning disk. The

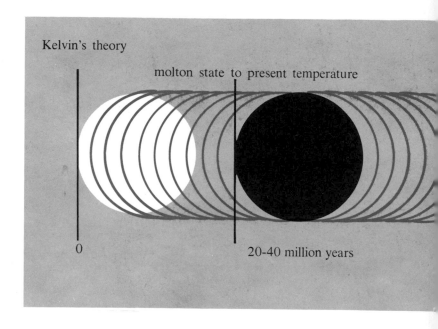

Kelvin's theory

molton state to present temperature

0

20-40 million years

central part of the disk rotated more slowly than the outer parts and this became the sun. The faster moving particles of the outer rings gradually accumulated into larger masses of gas, molten material, and dust. These bodies eventually cooled and solidified to become Earth, Mercury, Venus, Mars, Jupiter, Saturn, Uranus, Neptune, and Pluto — the planets of our solar system.

No one knows exactly when the solar system was formed, but we do know that it happened many *billions* of years ago. It is thought that the original swirling mass of dust particles that gave rise to the solar system may have originated as many as 10 billion years ago. The planets themselves came into being much later—possibly within the last 5 billion years.

Because we will probably never find the very first rocks that formed on the earth, we may never know the exact age of the earth. Scientists have, nevertheless, discovered some extremely ancient rocks—rocks that are known

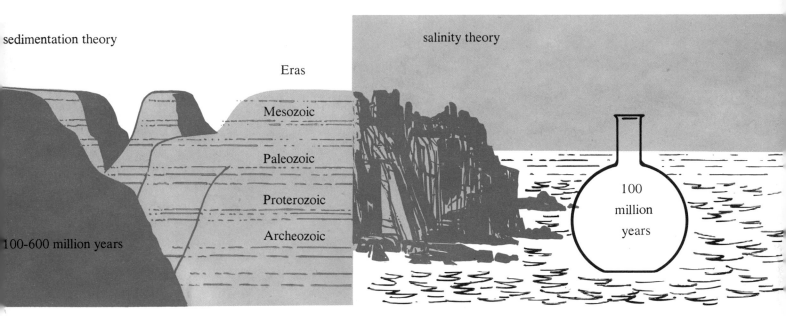

sedimentation theory

Eras

Mesozoic

Paleozoic

Proterozoic

Archeozoic

100-600 million years

salinity theory

100 million years

to be more than 3 billion 300 million years old! Found in South Africa, these are the oldest rocks that have yet been dated.

Perhaps you are wondering how it is possible to tell the age of a rock. This has been done by several different methods. Some of these have proved to be surprisingly accurate but others provide only a rough estimate of the earth's age.

Lord Kelvin, the famous British physicist, made one of the earlier scientific attempts to determine the age of the earth. Proposed near the end of the nineteenth century, his theory was based upon the assumption that the earth must have cooled to its present state from an original molten condition. Kelvin believed that since the approximate rate of cooling and the present temperature of the earth could be measured, the entire period of cooling could be calculated. Dated by this method the earth is believed to be 20 to 40

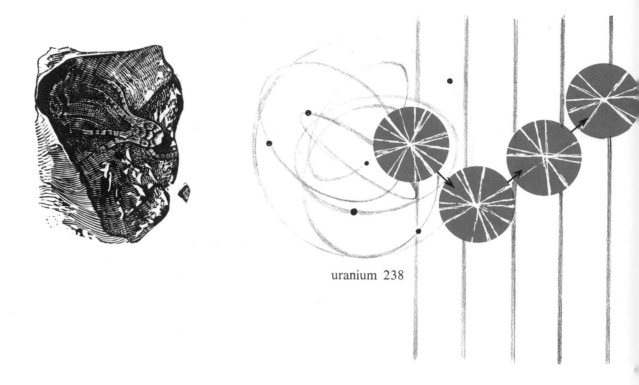

uranium 238

million years old. Although considerably more accurate than the 6,000 year date of Creation estimated by some biblical scholars, Lord Kelvin's method has also been discarded.

Scientists next attempted to determine how long it has taken to deposit all of the rock layers in the earth's crust. They first conducted experiments to learn how long it took to deposit one foot of sediment. Then they tried to find the maximum thickness of rock deposited during each period of geologic time. These thicknesses were then added together to give some idea as to the age of the earth. Age estimates derived by this method range from 100 to 600 million years.

Another approach was to try to measure age by the amount of salt in the ocean. It is assumed that the oceans were probably originally composed of fresh water. They became salty as salt was dissolved from rocks and soil and added to the sea by streams. If, said the scientists, we can determine how

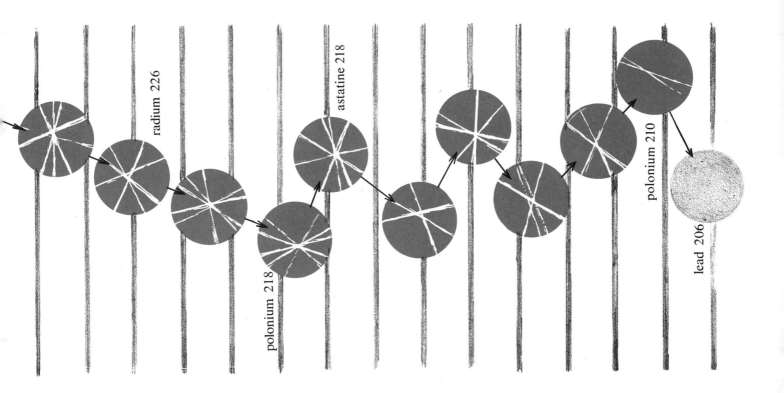

radium 226

astatine 218

polonium 218

polonium 210

lead 206

much salt is in the sea today and how much is added each year by rivers, we should be able to calculate how long this process has been going on. Figures derived from these calculations indicate that it probably took about 100 million years for the sea to reach its present degree of salinity.

Each of the above methods was an improvement over earlier attempts at estimating the age of the earth and each had many strong supporters. But, unfortunately, all of these methods depend upon estimates, average rates, and other uncertainties and guesses. For this reason they have been rejected by most of our present-day scientists.

Luckily, however, these unreliable methods have been replaced by a method of dating that is both practical and accurate. This technique is made possible because of the *radioactivity* of certain minerals which are found in the earth's crust. It is known that chemical elements that are radioactive break down into lighter elements at a definite rate. This rate remains constant and is not affected by changes in heat, pressure, chemical conditions, or the passage of time. Thus, when a radioactive element such as uranium decays, helium (a gas) is released and a series of new elements is formed. The last substance formed in this series is the element lead. By calculating the ratio between the radioactive lead and the remaining amount of uranium present in a given specimen, it is possible to determine how long ago the radioactive rocks were formed. Tests made by this method, which can be used only on rocks contaning radioactive elements, indicate that the oldest rocks that have been dated thus far were formed about 3 billion 330 million years ago.

The method described above is fine for dating extremely ancient rocks but cannot be used to date rocks of less than about 10 or 15 million years of age. But in 1947, Dr. Willard F. Libby, former chief of the Atomic Energy Commission, and his associates at the University of Chicago developed a dating technique that is reliable for measuring relatively short periods of geologic time. Called *radiocarbon dating*, this method has proved most successful in dating objects less than 40,000 years old.

Briefly, this method is based on the fact that all organisms contain a constant amount of radioactive *carbon-14*, or *radiocarbon*. When a plant or animal dies, radiocarbon is gradually turned into nitrogen. This process proceeds at a definite rate so that one-half of the carbon-14 has decayed at the end of about 5,570 years (the so-called *half-life* of carbon-14). The approximate age of an object may thus be determined by comparing the amount of radiocarbon remaining in the object to the amount present in most living things.

Radiocarbon is extremely useful in dating archeological objects such as bits of hair, fabric, bone, shell, wood, and charcoal. Among the more important objects dated by this method are the famous Dead Sea scrolls. Discovered in 1947 in a cave west of the Dead Sea near modern Jericho, these 11 scrolls represent seven independent works. They are of particular interest to Bible scholars for one of the scrolls contains the complete Book of Isaiah. By means of radiocarbon tests, the scrolls have been dated back to 33 A.D., with a possible margin of error of 200 years in either direction.

In recognition for his outstanding work with radiocarbon dating, Dr. Libby was awarded the 1960 Nobel Prize in chemistry.

The bands above give some indication of the geologic range and relative abundance of the major groups of plants and animals. An increase in the width of the range band corresponds to a relative increase in numbers during the corresponding portion of geologic time.

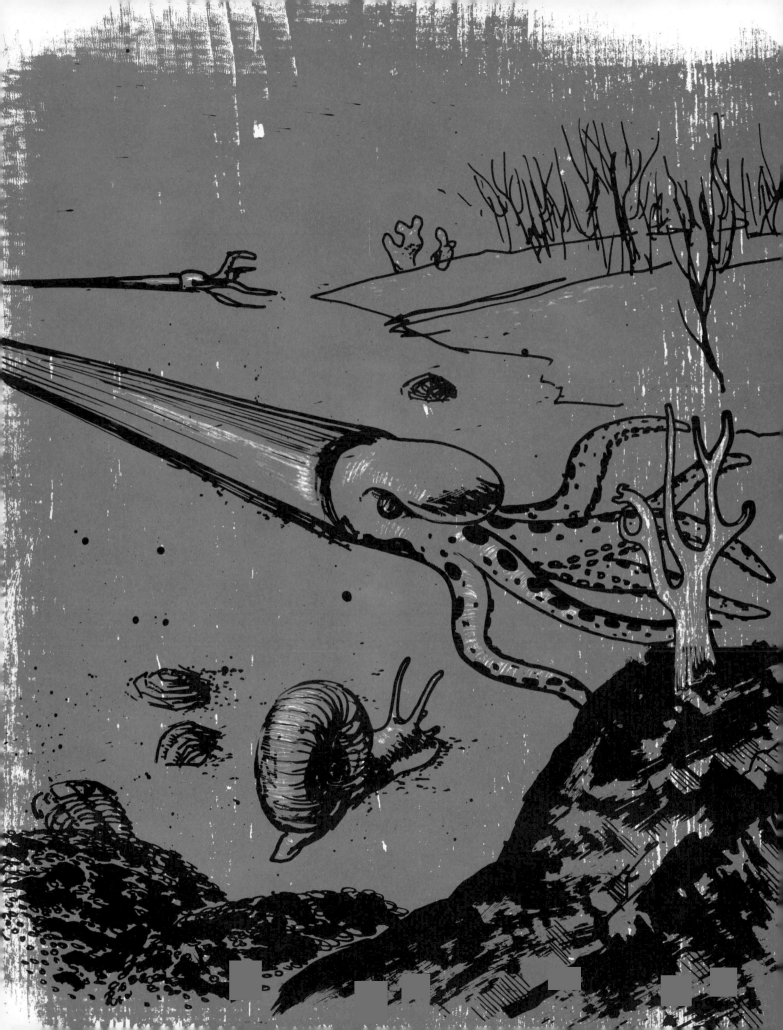

THE
GEOLOGIST'S
CALENDAR

The earth historian, like the historian dealing with the development of civilization, must have some method of relating important events to each other. For this purpose the geologist has devised a special *time scale* composed of large and small units of geologic time.

But unlike days and years, the units of the time scale are arbitrary and of unequal duration. For this reason we cannot be certain as to the exact amount of time involved in each unit. The largest units are called *eras* and each era is divided into smaller units called *periods*. A period of geologic time is divided into *epochs,* which, in turn, may be subdivided into still smaller units. Arranged in the order of their age, these units form a giant geologic "calendar" which provides a standard by which one can discuss the age of fossils and their surrounding rocks. By referring to the time scale, it is possible, for instance, to state that a certain animal lived during the Paleozoic era in the same manner that a historian might speak of a general who served during the Civil War. Each of these time terms gives us some idea as to the relative time when the animal lived or the general served.

We have already learned that the earlier "chapters" of earth history are written in the older rocks and are thus located at the bottom of the scale. Because of this, the time scale is always read from the *bottom* of the scale upwards.

Cenozoic	Quaternary
	Tertiary
Mesozoic	Cretaceous
	Jurassic
	Triassic
Paleozoic	Permian
	Pennsylvanian
	Mississippian
	Devonian
	Silurian
	Ordovician
	Cambrian
	Precambrian

Carboniferous

Animals and when they lived

As you look at the time scale you may wonder why some of the units have been given such unusual names. Why not use simple English words that would be easy to spell and pronounce? The answer to this lies in the words themselves. Many of the names of the time units have been derived from Greek and Latin words. There are good reasons for this. First, ancient Latin and Greek are "dead" languages and do not change the way modern English does. Second, they are "international" languages that mean much the same to scientists all over the world. The word *Paleozoic,* for example, comes from the Greek words *palaios* meaning "ancient" and *zoikos,* pertaining to "life." This is the geologist's way of saying that Paleozoic time was the time of ancient life. This is all expressed in a single word that can be understood all over the world.

The other eras, the Archeozoic, Proterozoic, Mesozoic, and Cenozoic, mean "beginning life," "primitive life," "middle life," and "recent life."

Archeozoic and Proterozoic rocks are commonly grouped together and referred to as *Precambrian* in age. The Precambrian rocks have been greatly contorted and changed and the record of this portion of earth history is most difficult to interpret. Precambrian time represents that portion of geologic time from the beginning of earth history until the deposition of the earliest fossil-bearing Cambrian strata at the beginning of the Paleozoic era. If the earth is as old as is believed, Precambrian time may represent as much as eight-five per cent of all geologic time.

As mentioned earlier, the eras have been subdivided into smaller units of geologic time called periods. Most of the periods derive their names from the places in which the rocks of the period were first studied. Thus, Devonian rocks were named for the county Devonshire in England and the Pennsylvanian for rock exposures in the state of Pennsylvania.

While the units discussed above are the major divisions of geologic *time,* the geologist usually works with the smaller units of *rocks* called *formations.* A geologic formation is identified and established on the basis of definite physical and chemical characteristics of the rocks. Formations are usually given geographic names which are combined with the type of rock that makes up the bulk of the formation. For example, the Beaumont clay was named from clay deposits that are found in and around Beaumont, Texas.

FOSSILS-
SILENT
WITNESSES
OF
THE
PAST

In August, 1900, a Russian hunter trudged along the Beresovka River Valley in eastern Siberia. Suddenly he stopped. He could hardly believe his eyes. Yet, there it was—the head of an elephant sticking out of the frozen soil beneath his feet!

We cannot blame the hunter for being shocked. After all, who would have expected to find the remains of an elephant 60 miles inside the Arctic Circle and more than 2000 miles north of the normal range of modern elephants? Anxious to report this improbable find, the hunter hurried back to his village. But before he left he chopped off one of the elephant's tusks— surely no one would believe his story unless he brought back proof!

News of the frozen elephant created much excitement among the villagers and they were especially interested in the ivory tusk. The hunter soon sold the ivory to a Russian soldier through whom news of the Beresovka elephant eventually reached scientific authorities in St. Petersburg (now Leningrad).

Anxious to investigate such an unusual discovery, the National Academy of Sciences organized an expedition to collect the specimen. Finally, after a journey of about 3000 miles, the scientists reached the locality where the elephant had been found. Thirteen months had passed since the remains were first reported, and part of the flesh had decayed and some had been eaten by wild animals.

Undismayed, the men began to dig the frozen soil away from the elephant's carcass. Imagine their surprise when they discovered that much of the animal's flesh was so perfectly preserved that it was hungrily devoured by the expedition's sled dogs! They were even more surprised when they studied the creature's physical characteristics. Unlike our living elephants, this unusual beast had a body covering of thick, coarse hair and a warm underlining of woolly fur. The scientists, then knew that the hunter had found a woolly mammoth, a type of extinct elephant that roamed over much of Eurasia and North America tens of thousands of years ago!

Although most fossil discoveries are not so exciting or unusual as those of the frozen mammoths, many of them are equally important. For each time a new fossil is discovered and described we add a page to the history of the development of life on earth.

Unfortunately, however, fossils have not provided us with the answer to one of the most important questions of the history of life: How did life begin? As yet, man has not learned how life started or where it came from. But it is known that life has been present on our earth for more than a billion years—far longer than anyone once dared to imagine.

We have also learned that the first plants and animals to inhabit our earth were rather unlike those of today. These early organisms were relatively simple and primitive. But with the passage of time, these early forms became increasingly complex and gave rise to plants and animals more like those of our modern world.

As life evolved, many different kinds of plants and animals lived and died. Some, like the dinosaurs, flourished but a relatively short time and then vanished from the face of the earth. Others such as the algae (simple one-celled plants) have remained virtually unchanged for more than a billion years.

Reprinted by permission from
*Fossils—An Introduction
to Prehistoric Life*, by
W. H. Matthews III, Barnes &
Noble, Inc., New York.

Most organisms, however, have changed during the course of their development. Consequently, those living during any given time were different from those living in earlier or later times. Thus, the marchers in the parade of life have left behind them a good record of the development of life —a record that is interpreted by means of fossils.

Fossils have provided us with most of what we know about life of the geologic past. Although they were not thoroughly understood, fossils attracted man's attention very early. It appears that even the "cave men" were interested in fossils, for the teeth and shells of prehistoric animals have been found associated with the bones of certain of these early humans. Of course, primitive man did not collect fossils in order to learn about prehistoric life. On the contrary, he probably regarded those relics of past life with supersti-

Mythical Phoenix, a bird
34
accredited with supernatural powers,
sacred to the Egyptian sun god, Ra.

tion and fear. It is also possible that early man believed that fossils possessed certain supernatural powers. They could thus be used for purposes of healing or to remove curses. In fact, this belief persists among some primitive cultures today. Certain tribal medicine men include fossils among the many strange objects found in their "healing" kits. Fossil bones and teeth are commonly found in Chinese druggists' shops where they have been pulverized and used in certain medications and "healing potions."

There is also evidence to suggest that some early Greek scholars were almost as confused as the "cave men." For example, the great Greek naturalist, Aristotle, recognized fossil fish as the remains of fish but he was not sure how they got in the rocks. He thought that they had been formed by certain mysterious "plastic forces" at work within the earth. One of his students, Theophrastus, had a different idea. He believed that either the fish had wandered into the earth by means of underground rivers, or that fish eggs had been left in the rocks to hatch at some later time! We should not judge these explanations too harshly, however, for these men lived more than 2200 years ago.

Fossils also attracted the attention of the great Greek historian, Herodotus. He noted the presence of small fossils known as *nummulites* (the remains of one-celled animals called *foraminifers*) in certain Egyptian limestones. These small fossils are shaped like lentils, little lens-shaped edible plants related to the pea. These, said Herodotus, are petrified lentils that were left over from the food supplies of the slaves who built the pyramids! Later, however, Herodotus noticed the presence of fossil shells and fish in the Egyptian desert and correctly stated that the Mediterranean Sea had once covered that area.

During the so-called "Dark Ages," fossils were thought to be freaks of nature or devices of the devil which had been placed in the rocks to lead man astray. Unfortunately, these superstitious beliefs hindered the study of fossils for hundreds of years.

In approximately the middle of the fifteenth century, the true origin of fossils was accepted and they were considered to be the remains of prehistoric organisms which had been preserved in the earth's crust. Certain scientists of this period correctly stated that fossils were the remains of marine organ-

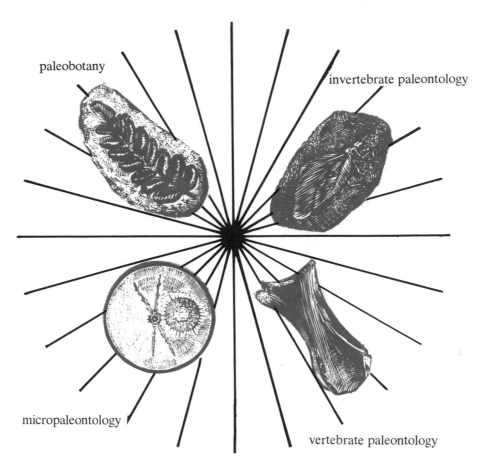

paleobotany

invertebrate paleontology

micropaleontology

vertebrate paleontology

Divisions of Paleontology

isms which had been brought in by prehistoric seas which once covered the area. But this explanation was not generally acceptable. Many people still explained fossils by myths or as the remains of monsters, dragons, and giants.

Among the early scientists who would have no part of such superstitious explanations was Leonardo da Vinci. He believed, and rightly so, that the fossils he found in Italy were the remains of animals that had once inhabited prehistoric seas and had been buried in the sediments of the sea floor. Then, much later in earth history, the ocean bottom had been raised well above sea level to form the Italian peninsula.

In the late eighteenth and early nineteenth centuries, fossils finally were recognized as relics of prehistoric life. Since that time fossils have become increasingly important in determining the succession of life on earth.

The study of fossils has greatly increased our knowledge of ancient plants and animals and of the world in which they lived. This is not surprising, for there are all types and sizes of fossils. Some are gigantic—a single dinosaur bone may be more than six feet long and weigh almost 600 pounds! Other fossils are so small that more than one hundred would fit on the head of a pin and you could not even see them!

Because there are so many different kinds of fossils, paleontologists have divided their science into four main divisions. These include: *paleobotany*—the study of fossil plants and the record of the changes which they have undergone; *invertebrate paleontology*—the study of fossil animals without backbones or spinal columns (clams, snails, worms, etc.); *vertebrate paleontology*—the study of fossil animals with backbones or spinal columns (fish, dinosaurs, woolly mammoths, etc.); and *micropaleontology*—the study of microfossils (fossils so small that they are best studied under a microscope). Each of these branches of paleontology has made important contributions to the unraveling of the mysteries of prehistoric life.

Although the remains of many different living things have been entombed in the rocks, only a minute fraction of prehistoric organisms have left any record of their existence. When plants and animals die they usually decay and disappear. If, however, they have some hard parts, such as teeth, shells, or bones, there is a better chance that fossilization might occur. It is also important that the plant or animal remains be covered by some type of protective material shortly after death.

The type of material burying the remains usually depends upon where the plant or animal lived. Thus, the remains of marine animals are commonly preserved because they fall to the ocean floor soon after their death. There they will be buried by soft muds which will be the shales and limestones of later geologic periods. In general, the finer the sediment, the better are the chances that the remains will be preserved. The finer sediments are less apt to damage the remains, and certain fine-grained limestones in Germany have faithfully preserved such delicate specimens as insects, birds and jellyfishes.

In some areas, plants and animals living near volcanoes have been covered by volcanic ash or dust. In Yellowstone National Park there is a whole forest which had been buried in this manner. The trees are in an excellent state of preservation and many still stand erect as if growing!

HOW FOSSILS ARE FORMED

In the city of Los Angeles, there is an ancient graveyard which has yielded hundreds of thousands of fossil bones! Where did all of these bones come from? Let us pretend that we are in the State of California. But not the California of today. Imagine, instead, how this state might have appeared more than 100,000 years ago. We would have seen no sprawling cities, busy freeways, or colorful orange groves. Instead, the countryside was populated by huge, lumbering elephants, clumsy, shaggy ground sloths, snarling saber-toothed cats, and howling wolves.

In what is now Hancock Park in Los Angeles, there were springs of petroleum bubbling on the surface. With the passage of time, the oil in these springs changed into tar. Sometimes these tarry pools would be covered over by blowing sand or a shallow film of water, thus converting them into natural animal traps.

Unsuspecting animals in search of water might easily have mistaken one of these water-covered tar seeps for an ordinary pool of water. When they moved in for a drink they soon became stuck like flies on fly paper! One can easily imagine the frightened trumpeting of a trapped woolly mammoth attracting such vicious beasts as the saber-toothed cat. Never one to pass up an easy meal, the great cat would have undoubtedly pounced upon the unfortunate elephant only to become trapped himself! Even the vultures, which must have hovered above such a scene in great anticipation, often became mired in the tar. We know this for the bones of these large birds are found mixed with the remains of the other unfortunate creatures which met their fates in the California tar pits.

Preservation in tar is but one of the many ways in which organisms may become fossilized. Some, like the woolly mammoths, have been kept in "cold storage." Others, such as petrified trees, have literally turned to stone, and some have been left as a thin film of carbon.

The way in which an organism becomes fossilized usually depends on the original composition of the organism, where it lived, and the forces that affected it after death.

In order that we might have a better understanding about how fossils are formed, let us briefly review the various types of fossil preservation.

The fleshy parts of organisms have been preserved under very special conditions. It is under such circumstances that the well-preserved woolly mammoths have been found in the frozen tundra of Alaska and Siberia. These huge beasts, which have been buried for more than 25,000 years, have been exposed as the earth begins to thaw. In this way, muscle, hair, skin, internal organs, and even clotted blood have been preserved! You can see the original hair and skin of some of these elephants in some of our larger museums today. One museum actually has part of a mammoth in a special freezer, and several display muscle and internal organs preserved in alcohol.

There has been much speculation as to how these great elephants died and became buried in the ice. One theory is that they may have fallen into great crevasses (cracks) in the ice or frozen ground. Some of the mammoths have been found with unchewed vegetation clenched between their teeth and

*Prehistoric insect
so well preserved
in amber that even
delicate tissues
are discernible.*

many show evidence of broken bones. This lends support to the idea of a sudden and violent death for these creatures.

Frozen mammoths have been of more than mere scientific value. Over the years, the natives of Siberia have collected the tusks of more than 50,000 of these extinct elephants and sold them to ivory traders!

In rare instances, soft parts of animals have been preserved in oil-saturated soil. One such fossil, the well-preserved nose-horn, foreleg, and part of the skin of an extinct rhinoceros, was found in eastern Poland in 1907. The body of this creature was completely encased in a waxy covering which prevented decomposition of the soft parts.

One of the more interesting and unusual types of fossilization is preservation in *amber,* or fossil resin. This occurred when prehistoric insects became stuck in the thick resin which seeped out of ancient cone-bearing trees. With the passing of time, the resin hardened leaving the insect encased in a yellow tomb of amber. Some insects and spiders have been so well preserved that even fine hairs and muscle tissues may be studied under the microscope. In some instances, such delicate material as fossil spider silk has been preserved in this manner.

During the more than 30 million years that they have been entombed, some of these insects have become so dehydrated and shrunken that only traces of the original tissue remain. In this type of preservation, a delicate lifelike mold of the original insect is visible. Oddly enough, if the amber is dissolved, almost no trace of the original remains will be found.

On very rare occasions prehistoric animals have become mummified. These "natural mummies" are formed by *desiccation,* or drying. For example, in 1928 an unusually well-preserved ground sloth was found in the

41

Casts and molds

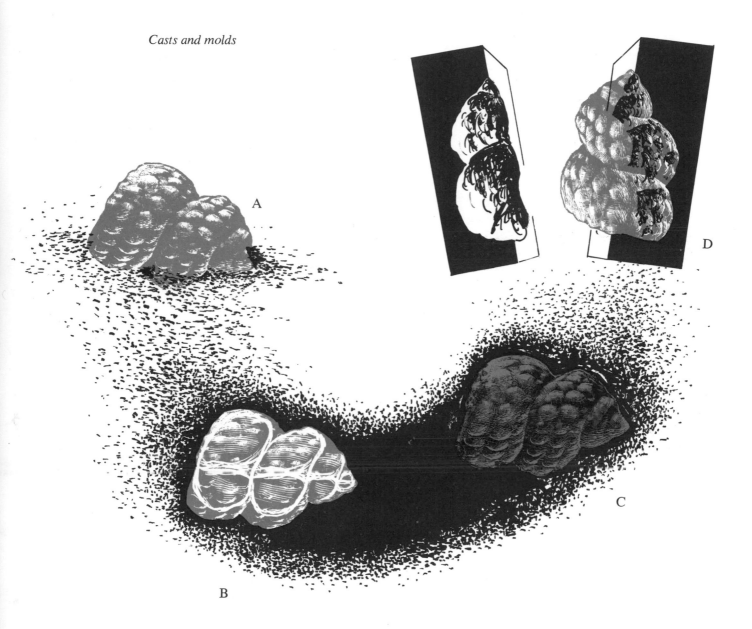

A. shell is covered

B. surrounding sand becomes rock mold

C. cavity fills to form a cast

D. mold and cast

crater of an extinct volcano in New Mexico. The animal apparently fell into the steep-sided crater and was unable to escape. It apparently died of starvation and the dry desert atmosphere caused dehydration of the body before decay set in. Further desiccation resulted in a natural mummy. The skeleton of this animal is complete, the bones being held together by the original sinews and tendons. Portions of dried skin as well as the claws are preserved. In rare instances, the skins of dinosaurs have also become mummified.

In 1910, Dr. Charles D. Walcott, a famous American geologist, was on a geologic expedition in Canada. As his party made its way slowly up the side of Mt. Wapta in British Columbia, the load on one of the pack animals shifted precariously to one side. As the group paused to readjust the slipping packsaddle, Dr. Wolcott's well-trained eyes spotted an unusual slab of black shale. The surface of this rock contained the outlines of several small creatures, many of which had not previously been found as fossils.

Sensing the importance of this discovery, the scientists and their assistants carefully worked their way up the side of the mountain in search of the source of this particular type of shale. After much careful prospecting, the shale bed was located some distance above the trail. There, embedded in rocks about 400 million years old, was a fantastic array of the remains of prehistoric organisms. Faithfully preserved as thin films of carbon were jellyfishes, worms, sponges, and seaweeds—forms not normally preserved even in younger rocks!

The fossils found by the Walcott party were preserved by *carbonization* —the same process by which coal was formed. This process, which is also called *distillation,* takes place as organic matter decays slowly after burial. During the process of decomposition, the organic matter gradually loses its gases and liquids, leaving behind a thin film of carbon which shows the outline of the organism.

An unusually fine degree of preservation may be attained by carbonization. "Carbon copies" of delicate fern leaves, the internal organs of invertebrates, and the fleshy parts of fishes and reptiles have thus provided valuable information about the soft parts of these organisms.

43

Although actual preservation and carbonization have produced some rather spectacular fossils, the paleontologist must usually work with remains that have been preserved in stone. Fortunately, most plants and animals have some type of hard parts which are capable of becoming fossilized. These may consist of the shell material of clams, oysters, or snails, the outer covering of crabs or corals, the woody tissue of plants, or the teeth or bones of vertebrates. Because these hard parts are composed of minerals which are capable of resisting weathering and chemical actions, fossils of this sort are relatively common. In many instances the hard parts have been preserved with little or no evidence of physical change.

The degree of preservation depends, in general, on the composition of the hard parts of the organism. Many invertebrates, such as clams, oysters, snails, and corals, have hard parts composed of *calcite* (calcium carbonate). The fossil shells of some of these forms are almost identical in composition to those of modern animals.

Other hard parts, especially vertebrate teeth and bones and the shells of certain invertebrates, contain large amounts of calcium phosphate. Because this compound is particularly resistant to weathering and chemical change, it is found virtually unaltered in fossils of all ages.

Many organisms possessing hard parts composed of *silica* (silicon dioxide) have become fossilized with little observable change. The siliceous hard parts of many microfossils and certain types of sponges have been preserved in this manner.

Some animals have an outer body covering (or exoskeleton) composed of *chitin,* a material similar in composition to our fingernails. The fossilized chitinous exoskeletons of certain insects, shrimps, and crabs have been preserved as thin films of carbon because of their chemical composition and method of burial.

More often, however, the hard parts of an organism have undergone some change. This is to be expected, for with the passage of time the original hard material will be considerably altered. Such changes may occur in a variety of ways, but the type of alteration is generally determined by the composition of the hard parts and where the organism lived.

44

As has already been mentioned, plant and animal remains are commonly petrified. Although the fleshy parts of an animal will not petrify, the hard parts may be converted into a stony reproduction of the original organic structure.

Sometimes the original hard material is slowly dissolved by ground waters and other minerals are deposited in its place. This process, known as *replacement,* may cause the original structure of the hard parts to be destroyed. However, some of the trees in the Petrified Forest which have been replaced by silica have the woody tissue reproduced in minute detail.

More commonly, however, fossils have become *permineralized.* This process occurs when porous bone, shell, or plant material becomes saturated with mineral-bearing ground water. The mineral content of the ground water is deposited in the cavities and pores of the hard parts with a minimum of alteration of the original structure. Remains preserved by permineralization are thus made heavier and more resistant to weathering. Many teeth and bones have been preserved in this way, as have large numbers of marine fossils.

But these are not the only types of fossilization. In addition to the preserved remains of plants and animals, certain traces of their existence are also considered to be fossils. In this type of preservation none of the original organic material nor any replacement of it remains. Instead, some trace or impression provides evidence of the plant or animal responsible for it.

For example, shells, bones, leaves, and other forms of organic matter are often preserved as *molds* and *casts.* Let us suppose that the shell of a prehistoric clam was pressed down into the ocean floor before the bottom sediments hardened. This would have produced an impression of the exterior of the shell. As time passed, the sediments turned to rock and the shell was completely encased in stone. Then at some later date in geologic history the shell decayed or was dissolved, leaving behind a cavity which is called a *mold.* A mold formed in this way will show the nature of the exterior of the shell and is thus called an *external mold.* If at some later time this mold was filled with another material, this produced a *cast.*

Tracks and trails also make interesting fossil evidence. Pliny Moody, a New England farmer, learned this in 1802. As he plowed on his farm near

South Hadley, Massachusetts, Farmer Moody unearthed an unusual piece of sandstone which was covered with peculiar birdlike tracks.

The tracks were numerous and of all sorts and sizes. These footprints created much excitement in the Connecticut Valley, and people came from miles around to speculate as what type of bird might have left them. No birds large enough to have made such tracks lived in the area, so where could they possibly have come from? News of the discovery eventually reached scientific circles and after much study the scientists declared the tracks to be those of a large flightless bird which no longer inhabited New England. It was 60 years later that the tracks were correctly identified as those of a bipedal (two-legged) dinosaur with birdlike feet!

Like the dinosaurs, most other animals have left records of their movements over dry land or the sea bottom. Some records, such as footprints, indicate not only the type of animal that left them but may also provide valuable information about the animal's environment. Thus, the study of a series of dinosaur tracks would not only indicate the size and shape of the foot, but also provide some idea as to the weight and length of the animal as well as its mode of walking. In addition, the type of rock containing the tracks would help determine the conditions under which the dinosaur lived.

Creeping and crawling invertebrates have also left tracks and trails. Such markings are not uncommon on the surfaces of certain sandstone and limestone deposits. These may be simple tracks, left as the animal moved over the surface, or the burrows of crabs or other burrowing animals. Fossil evidence of this sort provides information as to the way in which these animals moved and of the type of environment they inhabited.

The fossil burrows called *Daemonelix,* literally meaning the "devil's corkscrew," are especially interesting. These spiral-shaped structures are believed to be the burrows of an extinct land-dwelling beaver that once inhabited western Nebraska.

Among the more interesting types of "circumstantial" fossil evidence are *coprolites* and *gastroliths*. Coprolites, meaning "dung-stones," are fossil dung or body waste. Such fossil fecal pellets, found in association with the animals that made them, have provided much information about the food habits and anatomical structure of these organisms.

The coprolites of marine reptiles have been found to contain the remains of fossil squids, fish scales, and bones. A coprolite believed to be that of a fossil dog contained the teeth of a rabbit and a mouse, as well as the bones of other small mammals. "Dung-stones" found associated with the skeletons of ground sloths in New Mexico suggest that these now-extinct creatures ate Joshua trees and other desert plants. Without the information provided by the sloths' coprolites, we would not know what type of vegetation these great animals fed upon.

The exterior of certain coprolites bear markings such as grooves and spirals. These may provide evidence of unusual characteristics of the digestive tract of the animal making them.

Equally interesting are the highly polished, well-rounded stones called *gastroliths*. These stones, known also as "gizzard stones" or "stomach stones" have been found with the remains of certain extinct reptiles. They are similar to the pebbles and gravel found in the gizzards of birds. It is assumed that these stones were used to grind up the stomach contents of these reptiles, thus aiding in their digestion.

Gastroliths are especially common with the remains of plesiosaurs (a type of extinct swimming reptile). It appears that some plesiosaurs swallowed large numbers of these stones. The remains of one such specimen contained half a bushel of gastroliths, the largest of which was four inches in diameter!

Dinosaur tracks in Cretaceous limestone in bed of Paluxy Creek, near Glen Rose, Texas. Photograph courtesy of American Museum of Natural History. Permission to reproduce by R. T. Bird.

man

great apes

Old World
monkeys

New World
monkeys

tarsoids

PRIMATE FAMILY TREE

lemurs

arboreal insectivores

HOW
FOSSILS
GET
THEIR
NAMES

A great variety of plants and animals have become fossilized. If we are to study or discuss these widely varied forms, it is necessary to have some method of grouping together closely related fossils.

In order to do this, scientists have divided the organic world of nature into the plant and animal *kingdoms*. These, in turn, have been divided into large divisions called *phyla* (from the Greek word *phylon*, a race). Each phylum is composed of a large number of organisms with certain characteristics in common. For example, all animals with a spinal cord are assigned to the phylum *Chordata* (having a notochord or "back-string"). Each phylum is reduced to smaller divisions called *classes*, classes are divided into *orders*, orders into *families*, families into *genera*, and each genus is broken down into *species*. Thus, the common dog belongs to the genus *Canis* and the species *familiaris*; and all living men belong to the genus *Homo* and the species *sapiens*. It is obvious that there are a large number of variations among individual men and individual dogs, but the general characteristics of each group are quite similar. In the writing of a scientific name, the generic name should always start with a capital letter and the specific name with a small letter. Both names must be italicized or underlined.

The following table shows the similarity in classification of man, a dog, and a clam.

Unit	Man	Dog	Clam
Kingdom	Animalia	Animalia	Animalia
Phylum	Chordata	Chordata	Mollusca
Class	Mammalia	Mammalia	Pelecypoda
Order	Primates	Carnivora	Eulamellibranchia
Family	Hominidae	Canidae	Veneridae
Genus	*Homo*	*Canis*	*Venus*
Species	*sapiens*	*familiaris*	*mercenaria*

Because many fossils are quite similar to plants and animals that are living today, the paleontologist classifies and names fossils by the same method that is used to classify modern organisms. Established in 1758, this method of nomenclature (naming) is based upon certain well-defined rules which are carefully followed by scientists all over the world.

According to this system of nomenclature, the scientific name of an organism or fossil must have two parts: the *generic* name (name of the *genus*) plus the *specific,* or *trivial,* name (the name of the *species*). Thus, *Tyrannosaurus rex* is the scientific name of one of the better-known dinosaurs. This dinosaur, like most people, has two names. But according to this system, a person's name, such as *John Doe,* would be written *Doe john.* In other words, the dinosaur's "last" name or surname (*Tyrannosaurus*) is written first. This is the generic name, or *genus,* of the dinosaur. The given name or "first" name (*rex*) is written last and refers to the species of the dinosaur. It tells us what member of the genus it is; just as *John* tells what member of the *Doe* family John is.

These rules further state that the name should tell something about the plant or animal named, and that it must be formed by combining Greek or Latin words. The name *Tyrannosaurus rex* means "King Tyrant Lizard." Can you think of a better name for the most vicious reptile that ever walked the earth?

Why must the scientist use Greek or Latin instead of simply calling this creature "King Tyrant Lizard"? Because if the name has been derived from Greek or Latin, both of which are "dead" languages (not subject to change from modern usage), the names will remain the same forever. Moreover, Greek and Latin are the "international" languages of science; they are understood by scientists all over the world. Consequently, *Tyrannosaurus rex* is known by the same name in Mexico, Russia, France, or any other country; for scientific names are international in scope. Occasionally an English word will be Latinized to form a scientific name. Hence, the dinosaur *Yaleosaurus,* which translates as "Yale Lizard," was named after Yale University.

You will soon learn that scientific names are not especially difficult to say. Every syllable is sounded, and they are pronounced very much as they are written.

51

PLANTS AND ANIMALS— OLD AND NEW

Now that we have learned how living things are classified, we can become acquainted with some of the more important groups of plants and animals. To do this we shall meet both old and new forms of life—organisms that are still living today and types known only as fossils.

Why is the paleontologist interested in recent life forms as well as those of the geologic past? He believes that if we are to understand properly the many different types of prehistoric life, it is necessary to know something about the organisms that are living today. In studying fossils the paleontologist relies on the principle of *uniformitarianism*. This long word has a rather short definition. It means that *the present is the key to the past*—that ancient organisms lived under conditions similar to those of their nearest living relatives or the recent forms that they most closely resemble. Thus, although dinosaurs have been extinct for about 70 million years, we know a great deal about them. The nature of their skeletons indicates that they

A Devonian forest

54

were reptiles and we assume that these extinct creatures had many of the
same habits as certain reptiles that are living today. Consequently, the
paleontologist must know something about *biology* (the study of living
things) as well as geology.

In the next few chapters we shall consider some of the more important
groups of plants and animals which have left some sort of paleontological
record. For each of these groups we shall begin with the more simple
organisms and proceed to the more advanced forms. This will be done
in the approximate order of their appearance in geologic time. Thus, the
first plants and animals to be described are small one-celled forms. These
are not only the simplest forms of life, they are also believed to have been
the first organisms to appear on earth. The vertebrates, because of their
more complex body structure and relatively recent appearance, are discussed last.

A Jurassic lagoon

Because scientific workers do not always agree on exactly the same classification, the system used in this book is based on the latest ideas of several authorities. It is simple enough to understand, yet complete enough to help you become familiar with fossils.

In some instances the brief descriptions and illustrations of each group may be helpful in the preliminary identification of some of the more common fossils. You will also find the diagrams and figures helpful in understanding the more technical descriptions of fossils found in certain reference books.

Our survey of life history begins with a brief summary of the major groups of the plant kingdom. Particular attention is directed to those plants which have left some sort of fossil record.

Although often fragmental and poorly preserved, plant fossils have provided us with much information about the development of plant life on the earth. Certain fossil plants are also of considerable value as indicators of ancient climatic conditions, and their remains have played a large part in the formation of our vast coal deposits.

Plant fossils also provide us with our oldest evidence of life on earth. These ancient fossils consist of the remains of lower plants such as algae and fungi. They were collected in southern Ontario and are estimated to be about two billion years old!

There are several interesting but complicated systems of plant classification. For simplicity and convenience, we will divide the plant kingdom into two groups—subkingdom Thallophyta and the subkingdom Embryophyta which includes two large phyla, Bryophyta and Tracheophyta.

The thallophytes are simple plants without roots, stems, or leaves. They include the fungi, algae, and lichens. Although not particularly well represented in the fossil record, there are more than 115,000 species of thallophytes living today.

Some of the algae secrete calcium carbonate and are thus important as rock builders. As noted above, certain of these algae deposits are among the oldest fossil remains yet found. These calcareous algae are fairly common in certain Precambrian rocks.

The *diatoms*, another type of algae, secrete a shell of silica. The remains of these microscopic plants are commonly found as fossils. In some parts of the world there are thick deposits of fossil diatoms which cover many square miles. This material known, as *diatomite,* is used as a pottery glaze and in the manufacture of dynamite.

Represented by simple rootless plants like the mosses and liverworts, the bryophytes have left a very meager fossil record. Some scientists believe, nonetheless, that these may have been the first plants to inhabit dry land.

Before the plants could effectively conquer the land, they had to develop a means whereby water could be raised from beneath the earth's surface to the highest part of the plant. The tracheophytes are able to do this by means of a system of tubes called the *vascular system*.

gingko leaf fossil

This phylum has been divided into four major subdivisions, among which are many well-known living and fossil plants. Such important forms as the ferns, evergreens, hardwood trees, and all the flowering plants have been assigned to this phylum.

Among the more common and abundant fossil tracheophytes are the ferns, cycads, and the ginkgos. The latter, commonly known as the maiden hair tree, is called a "living fossil" because of its primitive characteristics. The ginkgo tree is native to China and Japan. The Japanese consider the plant to be sacred and plant it near their temples.

Included also in this phylum are such important "coal plants" as the scale trees, club mosses, and scouring rushes. They commonly occur in many of the world's great coal deposits, and their remains make up a large part of the coal.

The fossilized remains of animals are common in many sedimentary rocks. Of many different kinds, they range from the shells of tiny one-celled animals to the bones of gigantic dinosaurs. The fossils most commonly found, however, are the remains of invertebrate animals such as clams, snails, oysters, or corals.

Strange as it may seem, certain organisms possess various characteristics of both plants and animals. For this reason it is sometimes difficult to determine whether one of these organisms should be placed in the plant or animal kingdom. This problem has prompted some scientists to suggest that these "in betweens" be placed in a separate kingdom—the *Protista*. Members assigned to this group are primarily one-celled organisms. Many have a long geologic history but only a few have left a satisfactory fossil record.

Among those organisms considered to be protistans are such plants as algae, fungi, molds, yeasts, and mushrooms. Questionable animal forms include the radiolarians and foraminifers, both of which are quite useful to the paleontologist. But in this book we will recognize only the plant and animal kingdoms. Consequently, the organisms mentioned above are discussed in their respective places in the plant and animal kingdoms.

In the next two chapters we will meet some of the more interesting and unusual animals that lived in the geologic past.

RADIOLARIA

ANIMALS
WITHOUT
BACKBONES

Although they are not usually the most spectacular fossils, the remains of invertebrate animals are commonly among the most useful tools of the geologist. Let us now look at some phyla of animals without backbones that have provided us with a good fossil record.

The protozoans are the simplest form of animal life. Composed of only a single cell, most are so small that they can be seen only with a microscope. The typical protozoan has no shell or exterior body covering. Some, however, do have external hard parts that can become fossilized. Two types of shelled protozoans, the *foraminifers* and the *radiolarians,* are useful as microfossils.

Members of the order Foraminifera secrete tiny chambered shells. They lived, and still live today, in countless billions in the ocean. As these tiny creatures died their skeletons fell to the bottom of the sea and there formed thick deposits of limy mud. This limy mud was eventually converted into limestone and chalk. The famous White Cliffs of Dover along the English Channel are composed of chalk formed largely from the hardened skeletons of these microscopic creatures.

The foraminifers, commonly called forams, are predominantly marine organisms. Their shells may be composed of chitin, silica, or calcium carbonate. In addition, some forms construct a shell composed of sand grains or tiny mineral particles which are cemented together by a sticky substance secreted by the animal. Some species are so particular about the materials they use that they select only grains of a special size and color!

Not all forams are microscopic in size. You will recall that some of them were large enough to have been noticed by Herodotus. This ancient Greek philosopher thought that the lentil-like nummulites were "left-overs" from the lunches of Egyptian slaves. Some of those found in the limestones of Pyramids are more than two inches in diameter! However, most forams are no larger than a grain of sand and if you want to see them you will need a strong magnifying glass or microscope.

Protozoans of the order Radiolaria are also microscopic in size but they have a shell composed of silica. Their shells are unchambered and commonly of very intricate design. Billions of these tiny creatures float at or near the surface of the oceans and when they die their shells drift slowly to the ocean floor where they form thick deposits of *radiolarian ooze*. Rocks formed from these deposits are called *radiolarian earth*. Such rocks are used in the manufacture of filtering and insulating materials.

Because they are so fragile and so very small, radiolarians have rather limited use as fossils. They do, however, have a very long geologic history.

Unlike the one-celled protozoans, the members of phylum Porifera (the *sponges*) have bodies composed of many cells. They are, nevertheless, rather simple animals with no clearly defined mouth, organs, or nervous system.

The word Porifera literally means "to bear holes." This refers to the many small pores, or holes, that perforate the body wall of the sponge. These tiny openings are used to take water into the central body cavity of the animal. The sponge then removes food particles from the water and passes it out through a larger central opening in the body.

solitary coral

colonial coral

sponge spicules

Paleozoic sponge

Girtyocoelia

Most sponges live in salt water where they grow in colonies attached to the ocean floor. They vary considerably in shape and size, some are less than one inch in height. Others may attain a diameter of more than six feet! Living sponges secrete a skeleton which may be composed of calcium carbonate, silica, or a substance called *spongin*. These materials are commonly in the form of *spicules*—tiny hard parts that help support the soft tissues of the animal. The spicules may be scattered throughout the body or joined together to provide a rigid framework.

When the sponge dies, the soft parts of the animal decay and the hard spicules are scattered about on the ocean floor. These may later become fossilized. Although not particularly common as fossils, sponges are among the oldest known animal remains.

The coelenterates, or "hollow-bodied" animals, include such familiar forms as the jellyfishes, sea anemones, and corals. All are water-dwelling creatures and most of them live in salt water. The living animal is characterized by a saclike body cavity, a definite mouth, and tentacles which bear stinging cells. Some forms, such as the jellyfishes, have an umbrella-shaped body and are single, free-moving organisms. Others, like the colonial corals, are composed of many individuals living together in a colony.

The jellyfishes, members of class Scyphozoa, are composed of about ninety-eight per cent water. They have no hard parts and are not normally found as fossils. However, unusual finds, in the form of carbon residues or impressions in fine sediments, are occasionally reported.

61

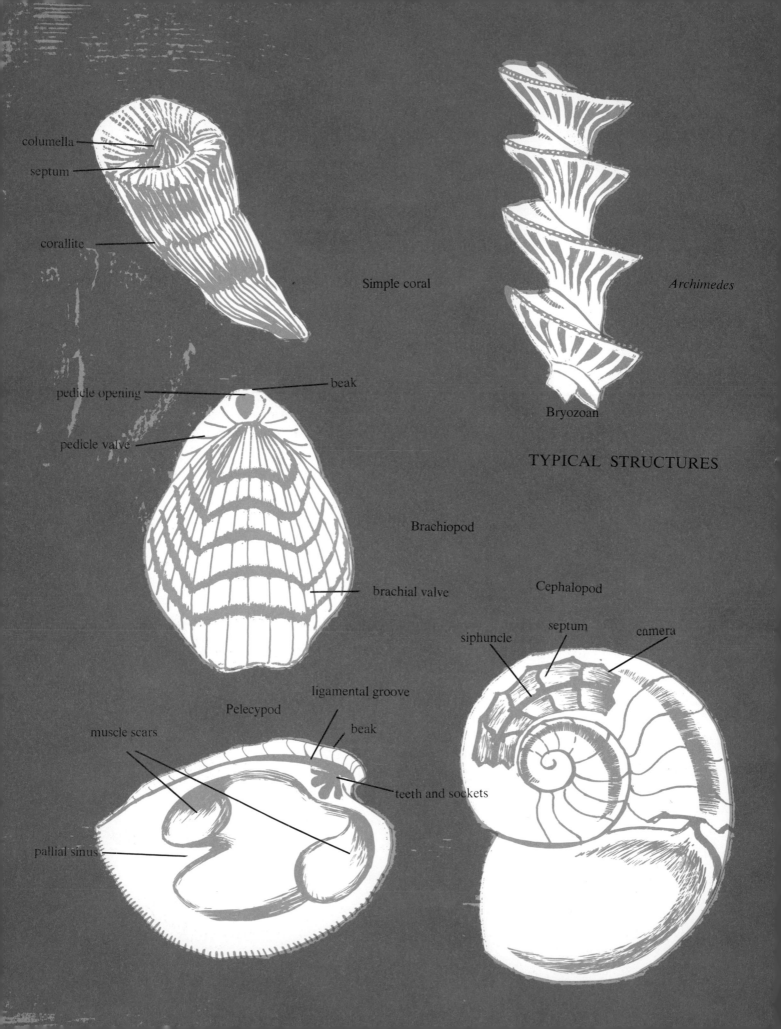

columella

septum

corallite

Simple coral

Archimedes

Bryozoan

TYPICAL STRUCTURES

pedicle opening — beak

pedicle valve

Brachiopod

brachial valve

Cephalopod

siphuncle   septum   camera

ligamental groove

Pelecypod

beak

muscle scars

teeth and sockets

pallial sinus

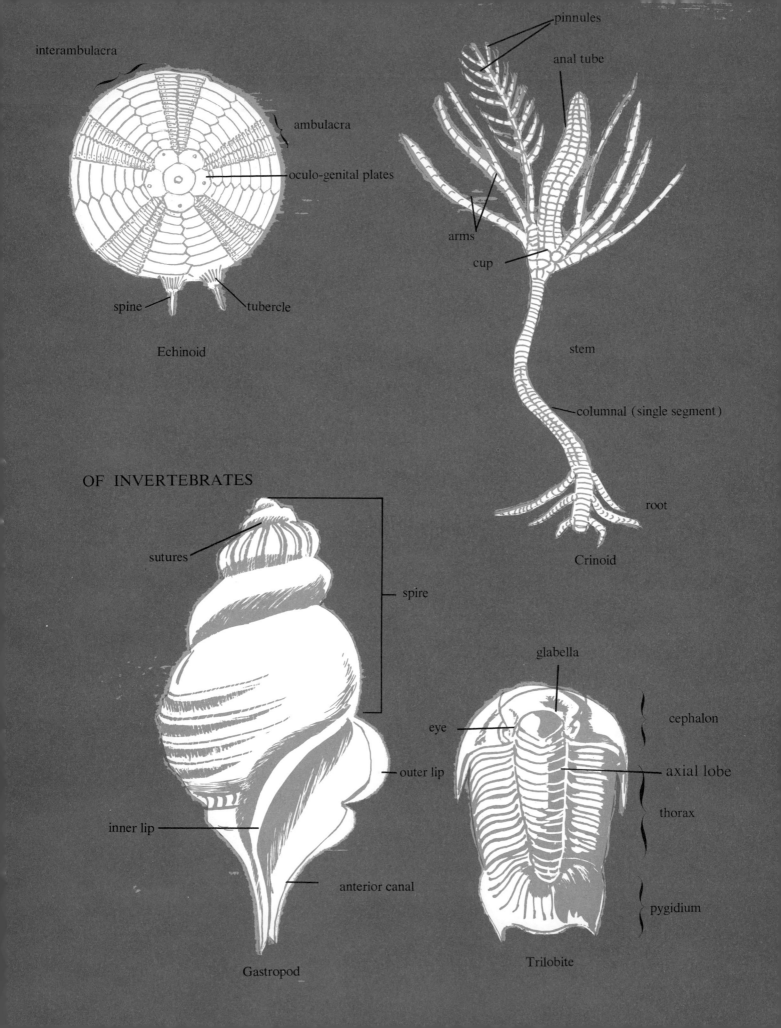

interambulacra

ambulacra

oculo-genital plates

spine   tubercle

Echinoid

pinnules

anal tube

arms

cup

stem

columnal (single segment)

root

Crinoid

OF INVERTEBRATES

sutures

spire

outer lip

inner lip

anterior canal

Gastropod

glabella

eye

cephalon

axial lobe

thorax

pygidium

Trilobite

On the other hand, the members of class Anthozoa are a very important group geologically. This class is composed of exclusively marine animals and includes the stony corals and the sea anemones. The mouth of the anthozoan is surrounded by a small circle of tentacles which resemble flower petals. Hence, these forms have been called the "flower animals." In fact, the name Anthozoa is derived from the Greek words for "flower" and "animal."

The coral animal, or *polyp,* secretes a cup-shaped *calcareous* (limy) exoskeleton. This skeleton, called a *corallite,* is usually divided by radial partitions called *septa* (singular *septum*). The polyp lives in the *calyx,* which is the central bowl-shaped depression in the top of the corallite.

Some corals build an individual corallite for each polyp. These are called *solitary* corals. Because of their shape they may be referred to as "horn corals," "cup corals," or "button corals." The *colonial* or *compound* corals join their little houses together to form one large stony colony. Some of these look like the horns of an elk, some are shaped like fans, and others look like a person's brain.

In tropical seas, coral colonies grow and add on to each other until large bodies called *reefs* are formed. The Great Barrier Reef off the northeast coast of Australia was formed in this manner. In North America such reefs are abundant at the southern tip of the Florida Keys.

Although coral remains have been found in rocks ranging from Ordovician to Recent in age, Paleozoic corals seem to be most commonly found. These include *Halysites,* a coral that is abundant in certain Silurian and Devonian rocks. In this form the individual corallites are arranged in a chainlike network. For this reason *Halysites* has been called the "chain coral." Another type commonly collected in Silurian and Devonian rocks is *Favosites,* the "honeycomb coral." The common name stems from the prismatic arrangement of the corallites which gives the colony a honeycombed appearance.

Fossil corals are especially helpful in providing information about prehistoric climatic conditions. Today corals typically live in waters associated with tropical and subtropical climates. So far as is known they have

Symmetry planes

Brachiopods

Rhynchotrema

Brachiopod

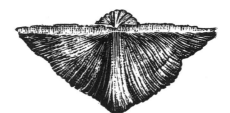

Mucrospirifer

Neospirifer

Dalmanella

Pelecypod

Juresania

Lepidocyclus

Lingula

always inhabited such waters. We therefore assume that the rocks which contain fossil corals were probably deposited in warm water. For example, fossil reef-building corals have been collected in the New Siberian Islands within the Arctic Circle. Their presence in this region suggests that the climate was tropical to subtropical in this area at least during Silurian time.

The little salt-water animals called bryozoans generally build stony skeletons of calcium carbonate. Because they are frequently found matted together on such objects as shells and stones they have been called "sea mats." Some species are branching and leaflike. Others resemble mosses and are thus called "moss animals," which is what the word Bryozoa means in Greek.

Among the so-called "stony" bryozoans each minute animal secretes its own limy house. These are joined together in colonies which somewhat resemble coral. However, the bryozoan animal is more advanced than the coral polyp. The bryozoan colony is covered with small holes, each of which is the home of a tiny animal. The colony may assume a variety of shapes; it may be lacy, branching, or moundlike. Some are even shaped like a corkscrew! The screwlike form has been named *Archimedes,* because it resembles the "Archimedes screw" developed by the early Greek mathematician. Archimedes developed this device to remove water from the holds of large ships. Similar screwlike machines are still used today in handling wheat and other grains.

In certain limestones of Mississippian age, the broken calcareous skeletons of bryozoans may make up the bulk of the rock. But although bryozoans are fairly common as fossils, they are rather difficult to identify.

Brachiopods are marine animals with shells composed of two pieces called *valves.* One of these valves is on the *ventral* (stomach) side of the body, the other is on the *dorsal* (back) side. The *pedicle valve* of some species has been extended into a *beak.* A hole, the *pedicle foramen,* is found in the beak of many brachiopods. A fleshy stalk called the *pedicle* was extruded through this hole; it was used to attach the animal to the sea floor. Some forms lose the stalk when they are fully grown. They then become attached by the ventral valve directly to the ocean bottom, or lie loose in the mud or sand. Others may be anchored to the bottom by spines.

66

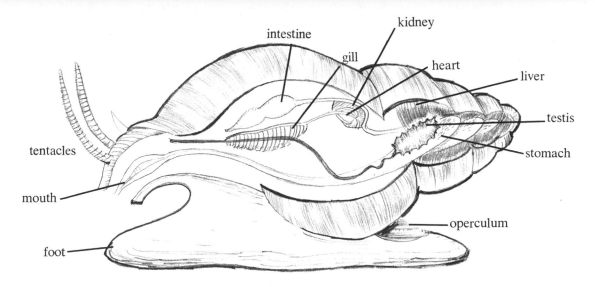

Section of a living gastropod

Murchisonia

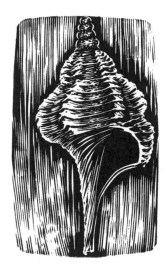

Fusus

Gastropods

Worthenia

Tylostoma

Bellerophon

The *brachial valve* is located on the dorsal side of the animal and is usually the smaller of the two. The valves are opened by means of strong muscles. Since these muscles relax when the animals die, fossil brachiopods are typically found with valves tightly closed.

The soft parts of brachiopods are composed of muscles, the *mantle* (which secretes the shell), and digestive, respiratory, reproductive, and excretory organs. There is also a tentacle-bearing structure called the *lophophore*. The place of attachment for such soft parts as the mantle, muscles, and lophophore can be seen in the interior of certain fossil shells.

The shape of some brachiopods resembles that of an early Greek lamp. For this reason, they are commonly called *"lampshells."* In general, however, brachiopods vary greatly in size and shape. They also exhibit a wide variety of ornamentation such as ribs, spines, knobs, growth lines, and other structures.

There are only two classes in this phylum. Class Inarticulata is composed of rather primitive brachiopods with a long geologic history. Their valves are held together by muscles and the shell does not have *teeth, sockets,* or a *hinge-line.* Members of class Articulata possess a well-defined hinge-line and there are teeth in one valve which *articulate* (join) with sockets in the opposite valve. Most brachiopods, both fossil and living, belong to this class.

Although there are only about 225 species of brachiopods living in modern seas, more than 15,000 species of extinct brachiopods have been described. Most of these lived during Paleozoic time. Fossil collectors who are hunting in exposures of fossiliferous Paleozoic rocks can normally expect to find large numbers of well-preserved brachiopods.

Two of the more common types of extinct brachiopods are the *productids* and the *spirifers.* The productids had spiny shells and were the largest, most abundant, and most varied brachiopods of the late Paleozoic. They are commonly found in Mississippian, Pennsylvanian, and Permian rocks.

The spirifers are sometimes referred to as "fossil butterflies" or "butterfly shells." This is an appropriate name as most spirifers have a wide wing-like shell and some species resemble a butterfly with pointed, outspread

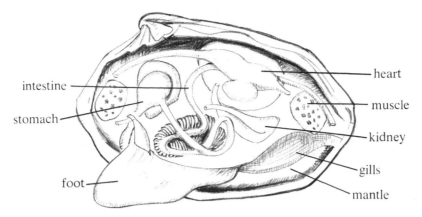

Section of a living pelecypod

Pelecypods

Trigonia

Exogyra

Glycymeris

69

Ostrea

Pecten

Exogyra arietina

Ostrea carinata

wings. Wide hinge-lines and prominent beaks are also typical of the spirifers. But probably their most characteristic feature is the deep groove, or *sulcus,* on one valve which matches a corresponding *fold* on the opposite valve. The different spirifers vary greatly in size, shape and ornamentation. They are especially common in certain Devonian formations.

This phylum is composed of a large number of invertebrates and includes such familiar forms as the snails, slugs, oysters, clams, squids, and octopuses. Two groups, the *ammonoids,* and the *belemnoids* are extinct. Their remains, however, are quite common as fossils.

Mollusks get their name from the Latin word *mollis* which means "soft." The soft bodies are covered by a thin, fleshy cloak called the *mantle.* The mantle is also used to secrete the hard calcareous shell that serves to protect the animal's soft parts. Fortunately, this shell is well adapted for preservation and mollusks are commonly found as fossils. However, some mollusks (the slugs) have no shell, and others (the squids) have an internal shell.

The lower part of the molluscan body is called the *foot,* a muscular structure that is designed for locomotion. The location and shape of the foot is a characteristic commonly used in the general classification of this group.

Because of their relative abundance and great variety, mollusks are particularly useful fossils. In addition, the remains of certain mollusks, such as the oysters, are important rock builders.

This large and varied group of animals has been divided into five classes:
1. *Amphineura*—the chitons or "sea-mice" which have a shell composed of eight pieces.
2. *Scaphopoda*—the "tusk-shells" with a single tubelike shell open at both ends.
3. *Pelecypoda*—the clams, mussels, oysters, and scallops, shells composed of two valves, usually, but not always, of equal size.
4. *Gastropoda*—the snails and slugs; slugs are without shells; snails have a single valved shell which is typically coiled.
5. *Cephalopoda*—the squids, octopuses, the pearly nautilus, and the ammonoids (extinct); shell of one valve partitioned by septa; extinct forms usually coiled.

70

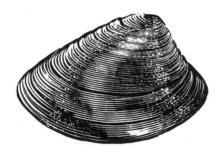

Exterior view of pelecypod shell (Nucula)

Of these five classes, only the Gastropoda, Pelecypoda, and Cephalopoda are particularly useful as fossils. These will be discussed in some detail. But because amphineuran and scaphopod remains are relatively rare, they are of limited use to the paleontologist.

Such familiar forms as clams, mussels, oysters, and scallops belong to class Pelecypoda. The pelecypods, a word which means "hatchet-foot" in Greek, have a muscular foot that resembles the wedge-shaped blade of a hatchet. Found in some of the oldest marine rocks known, pelecypods are still abundant in the seas, lakes, and rivers today. The majority of the "hatchet-footed" animals live in salt water and most are slow-moving forms that creep about the ocean floor. This type of pelecypod moves by means of the foot which is extruded between the open valves. Many of them burrow into the mud or sand, and some bore into wood, rock, or even other shells. Others, the oysters, for example, attach themselves to pilings, stones, and other objects. A few, such as the scallops, are able to swim by clapping the valves together and forcing out a jet of water through tiny holes in the hinge. This is a rather crude, but effective, type of jet propulsion.

The pelecypods, like the previously discussed brachiopods, are bivalves —their soft body parts are enclosed by two calcareous valves. The living animal is *aquatic* (water dwelling) and has well-developed soft parts. The fleshy mantle encloses the body and secretes the shell. In some forms part of the mantle is developed into the *incurrent* and *excurrent siphons*. Fresh water and food are brought into the *mantle cavity* by means of the incurrent siphons. Waste products are removed through the excurrent siphons. Respiration is by means of *gills* located within the mantle cavity. Of equal size and shape, the valves are located along the sides of the body. They are held together by a tough, elastic *ligament* which runs along the dorsal margin of the shell. Most forms also have a number of interlocking *teeth* and *sockets* which are located along the hinge-line. The teeth in one valve fit into those of the opposite valve to give strength to the hinge.

Although the general shape of the shell may vary greatly, most forms are typically clamlike. However, certain of these shells are round, others are long and narrow, and some have winglike structures. Pelecypods also vary

71

considerably in size. They range from tiny clams a fraction of an inch in length and diameter, to the giant *Tridacna* of the South Seas. The shell of this huge clam may attain a length of as much as six feet, a width of two feet, and a weight of several hundred pounds!

On the dorsal side of most pelecypod shells there is a *beak* which represents the oldest part of the shell. The beak is commonly located near the *anterior* (front) end of the shell. The end of the shell opposite this is designated *posterior* (the rear). The hinge and ligament are located *dorsally* (along the top) and the lower margin of the shell where the valves open is called *ventral*.

The inner surface of the shell bears certain markings which, along with the shell form and *dentition* (the nature and arrangement of the teeth and sockets), are important in classification. Muscle scars are present on the inside of most valves. These scars mark the place of attachment of muscles which were used to close the shell and aid in locomotion.

Along the ventral margin of some shells there is a line or scar which extends from the anterior muscle scar to the posterior muscle scar. Known as the *mantle line,* or *pallial line,* this structure marks the place where the mantle was attached to the shell. Although the soft parts have long been decomposed, these markings tell us something about the animal which lived inside.

The outside of the shell is usually marked by a series of *concentric growth lines.* These mark points where shell material was added as the animal grew. The external surface of many shells is also marked by various types of ornamentation. These include ribs, spines, grooves, ridges, nodes, and knobs.

Most of the pelecypod shell is composed of calcium carbonate, but the outer layer of each valve is composed of horny material. The inner surface of the shell is lined with a calcareous layer of pearly or porcelain-like material.

Many Paleozoic and Mesozoic pelecypods are found preserved as casts and molds, the soluble limy shell having been dissolved or eroded away. Certain Cretaceous and Cenozoic forms, however, may be found with the original shell perfectly preserved in an unaltered state.

Do not be surprised if you find only one valve of the pelecypod shell. When the animal died the muscles relaxed and the shells could easily become separated. But this does not always happen, for some fossil pelecypods are found closed and with both valves intact. If the animal died while burrowed in the mud, or is quickly buried by sediments, both valves may be found in place.

Members of class Gastropoda crawl on a single broad foot. Because the foot is located on the underside of the body, the animal appears to be crawling on its stomach. They are thus called *gastropods* which literally means "stomach footed." Snails, slugs, whelks, and conchs are all gastropods.

The most typical "stomach-footed" animal, the snail, carries a single-valved unchambered shell on its back. The animal can retreat into this shell when danger threatens. As an added precaution some univalves (shells with one valve) have a small trap door that they can close to keep out intruders. This little covering, called the *operculum,* is fastened to the upper surface of the foot. When the animal pulls in its foot the little trap door falls neatly into place, thus sealing off the opening to the shell.

Most snail shells are coiled into a spiral. Some, however, are cone-shaped, ear-shaped, wormlike, cylindrical, or screwlike. One group, the limpets, have an uncoiled shell shaped like a Chinese coolie hat.

Fossil gastropods are common in many Paleozoic, Mesozoic, and Cenozoic rocks. Consequently, most fossil collections contain a variety of well-preserved fossils of this type. In studying fossil gastropods it is helpful to know something of the *morphology* (structure or form) of their shells. The closed pointed end of the shell is called the *apex,* and each turn of the shell is call a *whorl.* The largest and last-formed whorl is called the *body whorl.* This whorl, which contains the *aperture* (opening to the shell), is the whorl in which the animal lives. The other whorls, exclusive of the body whorl, are known collectively as the *spire.* The inner and outer margins of the aperture are called *inner lip* and *outer lip,* respectively. Many of these structures may be used to distinguish one gastropod from the other.

Most gastropods live in shallow marine waters, but some inhabit fresh water. Aquatic forms have gills like fish, but the *terrestrial* (land-dwelling) forms breathe by means of simple lungs.

Certain *carnivorous* (meat-eating) snails have a rasplike tongue which is used for boring into other shellfish, which they eat. The neatly drilled holes made by these meat-eaters are found on many recent and fossil mollusk shells. Such holes are proof that carnivorous snails lived in the area even though their shells are not to be found.

Gastropod shells are normally rather easily dissolved. As a result, fossil gastropods are frequently preserved as casts and molds. This type of preservation occurs after the death of the animal, when the decay of the soft parts allows the shell to become filled with sediment. This filling later becomes solidified, and the outer shell may eventually be removed by weathering or solution. An internal mold of this type is called a *steinkern*. Such fossils generally do not provide much information about the exterior of the shell. It is not uncommon, however, to find fossil snails with the original shell in an excellent state of preservation.

Cephalopoda is Greek for two words that mean "head" and "foot." The members of this class are called "head-footed" animals because their foot is divided into many parts which always emerge from the head. Squids, octopuses, and the pearly nautilus are some cephalopods that live in modern seas.

The cephalopods are among the most advanced animals without backbones. They have highly developed nervous systems, eyes somewhat like those of humans, horny jaws, and many tentacles fused with the foot. All members of this class live in the sea and respiration is by means of gills.

Cephalopods have long been surrounded by myths and superstition. Both the huge, eight-armed octopus and the gigantic deep-sea squid have given rise to many weird sea stories. The latter are the largest known animals without a backbone. Living in the Atlantic Ocean off the coast of Newfoundland, some of these titans of the deep attain an overall length of more than 50 feet! They may weigh almost 30 tons. Their great serpentlike arms are covered with numerous sucker discs and may be as much as 35 feet long. It is not surprising that ancient seamen who observed these great tentacles at sea honestly believed that they had seen a "sea-serpent."

Both the squid and the octopus can swim by "jet propulsion." Water is taken into the mantle cavity and suddenly ejected through a structure known

74

Agnostus

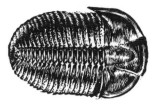

Elrathia

Eodiscus

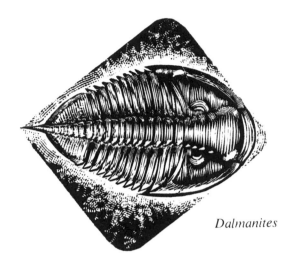

Dalmanites

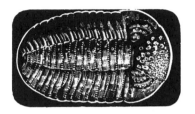

Phacops

TRILOBITES

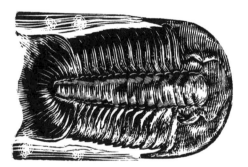

Dikelocephalus

Trinucleus

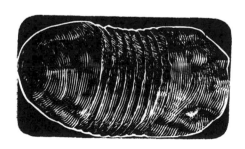

Bumastus

Flexicalymene

as the *funnel*. When the water squirts out of the funnel, the animal's body is pushed in the opposite direction. Squids have pointed tails and rudderlike fins which give them a streamlined appearance. Sometimes they move so quickly that they leave the water and shoot considerable distances into the air!

Squids and octopuses also have an *ink sac*. This structure is filled with a thick, dark-brown liquid. The ink can be thrown out into the water by the cephalopod thus providing the animal with cover to escape from enemies.

However, the two groups of cephalopods that are most likely to be found as fossils are both extinct. Both of these, the *ammonoids* and the *belemnoids,* died out at the end of Cretaceous time. But during the Mesozoic era the ammonoids were very abundant in the shallow seas that covered much of the world. Because their calcareous shells were well adapted to preservation and they were so numerous, ammonoids are valuable guide fossils for Triassic, Jurassic, and Cretaceous rocks. As in the case of all mollusks, the shell, if present, is secreted by the mantle. Most living cephalopods, such as the squids and the cuttlefish, have their shell inside their body. However, the more important fossil forms, the ammonoids and nautiloids, secreted an external calcareous shell. The only coiled cephalopod living today (the pearly nautilus) is found in the South Pacific. However, they lived in many parts of the world during the geologic past.

Among the externally shelled cephalopods found as fossils are forms which had straight, tapering, cone-shaped shells. Others had shells which were loosely coiled or coiled in a flat spiral like a ram's horn. Cephalopod shells differ from gastropod shells in that the shell is divided into a number of compartments or *chambers*. The chambers are separated from each other by calcareous partitions known as *septa*. The point where each septum joins the inner surface of the shell is called the *suture*. These *suture lines,* or *patterns,* are not visible from the outside unless the shell has been removed. However, they are visible on the internal molds of many fossil cephalopods.

In general, nautiloid cephalopods have very simple, smoothly curved patterns. The ammonoids are characterized by more complex and wrinkled sutures. Suture patterns are very useful in cephalopod classification, for different fossil forms possess distinctive and characteristic sutures.

As the cephalopod increased in size, it moved forward and developed new and larger chambers to fit the growing body; the older chambers were sealed off by the septa. In the living pearly nautilus, the abandoned chambers are commonly filled with gas which helps to keep the animal afloat while swimming. The last and largest chamber of the shell enclosed the animal's soft parts and is known as the *body chamber*. The opening into this chamber is called the *aperture*. A calcareous tube, the *siphuncle,* connected the living animal to the *protoconch,* the oldest part of the shell. The siphuncle passed through a hole in each septum. The above structures can be clearly seen on the sectioned shell of a pearly nautilus. Such shells are common in curio shops in many parts of the country.

Nautilus, the only living externally shelled cephalopod, is of considerable scientific interest. It provides the only living connection between the nautiloids and the ammonoids, and for this reason some scientists have referred to it as a "living fossil." It is interesting to note that the comparatively simple nautiloids have undergone relatively little change since the Early Paleozoic. The more complexly developed ammonoids, however, have been extinct for some 70 million years.

The earliest nautiloids were not coiled; their long, straight, slightly tapering shells had very simple suture patterns. These were especially common during Ordovician and Silurian time. *Endoceras,* an uncoiled Ordovician form, grew to be almost 20 feet long! Most, however, were much shorter.

Although in many ways similar to *Nautilus,* the ammonoid cephalopods are all extinct. They branched off from the nautiloids in early Devonian time, and became extremely varied and abundant during the Mesozoic era. But, like the dinosaurs which were so numerous at the same time, the ammonoids were extinct by the end of the Cretaceous period.

Ammonoids, like nautiloids, have shells that may be straight, partially coiled, or tightly coiled. But as mentioned earlier, these two groups of "head-footed" animals differ considerably in their suture patterns.

Nautiloid shells are typically rather plain but many of the ammonoids had shells ornamented in a variety of ways. Such structures as ribs, knobs, keels, and spines are common on many Mesozoic forms. Perhaps you are wondering why these structures can be seen on the internal casts of the fossil. This is because the ribs and knobs were not extra thicknesses of shell. Instead they appeared as hollows on the inside of the shell. When the animal died and the soft parts decayed, the hollow areas became filled with sediment. These are now seen as raised areas on the cast.

Some Cretaceous ammonoids coiled upwards into a spiral and their shells closely resemble those of certain high-spired Cretaceous gastropods. Do not mistake these spirally coiled ammonoids for gastropods. Look for suture patterns or other evidence of chambering—these will not be present in a snail shell.

Although the externally shelled cephalopods have left the most useful fossil evidence, certain of the internally shelled forms are also found as fossils. The *belemnoids,* representing the remains of extinct cuttlefish-like animals, are especially abundant in Jurassic and Cretaceous rocks. Belemnoids, or *belemnites,* as they are also called, were among the first fossils noted by man. Their sharp, dartlike appearance led to the superstition that they were "thunderbolts of the gods." During rainstorms they were commonly washed out of the surrounding rocks and left exposed after the storm had abated. When found by early man he assumed that these were darts or javelins that had been thrown down by his angry gods during the storm!

Of all the fossils for which the rockhound searches, none is more highly prized than the *trilobite.* A distant relative of the crabs and lobsters, this little three-lobed fossil is found only in Paleozoic rocks. The trilobite is a typical *arthropod,* a word literally translated as "joint-foot." Like all members of phylum Arthropoda the trilobites are characterized by jointed appendages and a segmented body.

Have you ever seen a horseshoe crab or king crab? This interesting creature has remained virtually unchanged since Paleozoic time and has been called a "living fossil." The trilobites resemble their distant cousins the horseshoe crabs in that they inhabited salt water and moved about by means of their jointed, leaf-like appendages.

Two grooves extend down the trilobite's back dividing it into three parts. The resulting three-lobed appearance gives the class Trilobita ("three-lobes-possessing") its name. The central, or *axial* lobe, runs down the middle of the body. The lobes on either side of the axial lobe are known as the *pleural,* or *lateral,* lobes.

Trilobites can also be divided into three parts from front to back. Beginning at the front is the *cephalon* or head. This part of the body contains the *cheeks,* the *antennae,* (or "feelers"), and the well-developed *compound eyes.* The part of the body behind the cephalon is called the *thorax.* It consists of from two to twenty-nine segments. In some species the thoracic segments join in such a way that the animal is able to roll up like the living sow bug or pill bug. Certain species are commonly found in this rolled-up position. The last or tail part of the body is known as the *pygidium.* This is usually formed from several body segments which are fused together.

The entire body of the trilobite was covered by an outer covering of chitin. The thicker top part, the *carapace,* is what is usually preserved as a fossil. The trilobite shed its skin or molted, frequently in order to grow, so each animal may have provided several fossils.

Trilobites had a wide variety of shapes and sizes. Certain Cambrian forms were only a fraction of an inch in length while one Devonian species reached a length of more than two feet! Most, however, were only two or three inches long.

These little three-lobed creatures first appeared in early Cambrian time, and were especially abundant during the Cambrian, Ordovician, and Silurian periods. Although trilobites formed about fifty per cent of the life of Cambrian time, they are not usually found in great numbers. Their relatively fragile carapaces have been subjected to considerable physical and chemical change and may be difficult to recognize. Trilobites become increasingly scarce in later Paleozoic formations and were extinct before the end of the Permian period.

Can you imagine a scorpion seven feet long? One group of extinct, "joint-legged" animals, the *eurypterids,* boasted a scorpion-like creature of this size. In life, certain of these giant arthropods had large pinching claws,

79

a stinger, and a poison gland. The eurypterids are even more closely related to the horseshoe crabs than are the trilobites. They are also close relatives of the ticks, scorpions, and spiders.

Among the other arthropods that are occasionally found as fossils are the crabs, insects, spiders, and barnacles. Insects and spiders have been preserved in amber and crab remains and barnacle plates are sometimes found in certain marine formations. Of particular interest to the micropaleontologist are the tiny arthropods called *ostracodes*. These tiny water-dwelling creatures have two shells, one on each side of the body. Externally they look very much like little clams. But the animal which inhabits the shell is a typical "joint-legged" animal with segmented body and "feelers."

All of the echinoderms, or spiny-skinned animals, live in the sea. They are appropriately named, for these creatures typically have a tough, leathery skin, with spines that range from a fraction of an inch to several inches in length. Included in this phylum are such familiar forms as the starfishes, sand dollars, sea cucumbers, and sea lilies.

The living echinoderms have well-developed nervous and digestive sysstems and a distinct body cavity. In general, their skeletons are composed of a number of limy plates which are neatly fitted together. Many echinoderms have star-shaped bodies or a star-shaped impression somewhere on their body. However, some of the "spiny-skins" are heart-shaped, biscuit-shaped, or cucumber-shaped.

Many echinoderms spend most of their lives attached to the sea bottom by means of a *stalk* or *stem*. Others, for example, the starfishes, are free-moving forms. Of the following classes the first three consist of attached forms. The members of the remaining three classes are all free-moving echinoderms.

1. *Cystoidea*—extinct, attached bladderlike echinoderms. They appeared early in Cambrian time and were extinct by the end of the Devonian period.
2. *Blastoidea*—extinct, budlike, attached echinoderms. Known as sea buds, they range from Ordovician to Permian in age.
3. *Crinoidea*—sea lilies; stemmed, lilylike echinoderms. Very abun-

dant during late Paleozoic time, but relatively scarce today.

4. *Stelleroidea*—starfishes and serpent stars; free-moving, star-shaped echinoderms. Not commonly found as fossils.
5. *Echinoidea*—unattached, spiny echinoderms, including sea urchins and sand dollars. Common fossils in certain Mesozoic rocks.
6. *Holothuroidea*—soft-bodied, sausage-like echinoderms called sea cucumbers. Rare as fossils.

The cystoids are the most primitive of the above-mentioned echinoderms. The cystoid body, or *calyx,* was not so well developed as that of the blastoid or crinoid. The body plates are irregularly arranged and the stem is short or absent. Relatively rare as fossils, they are locally common in certain Ordovician and Silurian rocks.

If you live in areas where there are outcrops of fossiliferous Mississippian rocks, perhaps you have found what many people call "fossil acorns" or "petrified nuts." It is not always easy to convince the local residents that these little blastoids are the remains of sea creatures that lived attached to the bottom of an ancient ocean that once covered the region. Because certain blastoids resemble somewhat the bud of a flower, they are commonly called *sea buds.*

Unlike the cystoids and crinoids, the blastoids had no arms. Some had stems, but others did not and they rested directly on the sea floor. The *mouth* is located in the middle of the calyx. It is surrounded by five small openings called *spiracles.* The spiracles, which were used to take water into the body, may be seen on many fossil specimens.

The oldest known blastoids first appeared about 500 million years ago during Ordovician time. They were especially abundant during the Mississippian period, and one species, *Pentremites,* is a valuable fossil guide to Mississippian rocks. Shortly thereafter they began a rapid decline and by the end of Permian time they were all extinct.

The only attached echinoderms living today are the *crinoids.* Commonly called sea lilies, the crinoids derive their name from their flower-like appearance. The stemmed calyx with its numerous branching *arms* resembles a long-stemmed flower. In life, sea lilies may be colored yellow, brown, purple, red, or lavender. They commonly grow together in "gardens" on the bottom of the sea where they resemble underwater flower beds. It is not surprising that early naturalists first thought them to be plants.

For a long time it was believed that the stalked crinoids, like the cystoids and blastoids, were extinct. But it is now known that these creatures occur in considerable numbers in the deeper waters of the Pacific and Indian oceans. However, they were much more abundant in ancient Paleozoic seas. Their remains occur in great numbers in many Mississippian and Pennsylvanian formations where they make up a large percentage of the rocks.

One group of crinoids, the *feather stars,* are attached only during their early life. When they reach the adult stage they become stemless and free-swimming. These forms are much more abundant than the more primitive stemmed types.

The skeleton of the sea lily is composed of three main parts; the *calyx,* the *arms,* and the *stem.* The calyx encloses the animal's soft parts and is composed of many regularly arranged limy plates. The typical crinoid calyx is cup-shaped with five grooves radiating out from its center. The mouth, which is located on top of the calyx, is surrounded by branched arms which help in gathering food.

A complete fossilized crinoid calyx is even more highly prized than a trilobite. Normally, however, the plates of the crinoid calyx became separated when the animal died. These then became scattered about on the sea floor and incorporated into the bottom sediments.

Crinoid stems, on the other hand, are commonly fossilized. Composed of a series of button-shaped disks called *columnals,* the stem was attached to the sea floor by a hooklike anchor or rootlike arms. An opening, the *axial canal,* is in the center of each columnal. In life this canal is filled with a fleshy stalk which provides food to the lower part of the animal. It also serves to hold the columnals together and provides flexibility for the stem. Some crinoids had stalks as much as 50 feet long. When the animal died the columnals became separated and sank to the ocean bottom. Some Paleozoic limestones contain such great numbers of crinoid columnals that they are called *crinoidal limestones.*

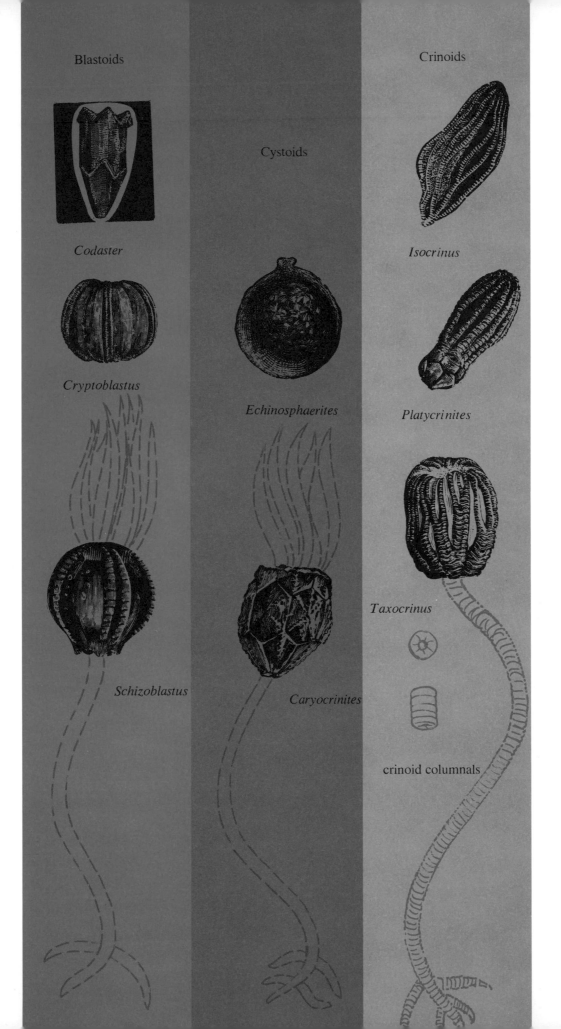

Blastoids

Cystoids

Crinoids

Codaster

Cryptoblastus

Echinosphaerites

Isocrinus

Platycrinites

Taxocrinus

Schizoblastus

Caryocrinites

crinoid columnals

Crinoid stems, very common fossils, may be known locally as "Indian beads," "pop rocks," "fish bones," or "petrified plant stems." Most crinoid columnals are shaped like little doughnuts or lifesavers. Others are four-sided, five-sided, many-sided, or oval-shaped.

Although the attached echinoderms have left a good fossil record, you are probably more familiar with the free-moving forms such as the starfish. Members of class Stelleroidea, which literally means "resembling a star," are typically star-shaped, free-moving echinoderms. Their bodies are generally divided into a central disk and five radiating arms.

More than 800 species of starfishes are living in modern oceans, but fossil starfishes are relatively rare. They do, however, have a long geologic history and range from Ordovician to Recent in age.

Sometimes called the "pincushions of the sea," the members of class Echinoidea are the spiniest of the "spiny-skins." Typical members of this class are the sea urchins and sand dollars. Like their first cousins, the starfishes, the echinoids are free-moving echinoderms. But unlike the starfishes, they are globular or disk-shaped rather than star-shaped. If you examine an echinoid closely, however, you will probably see a star-shaped impression on the upper surface of its body. This five-rayed starlike pattern marks the position of the *food grooves*. These are comparable to similar structures on the underside of the starfish arm.

The sea urchin's body is enclosed by a large number of closely fitting calcareous plates. The outer surface of the body is typically covered with movable spines which vary greatly in size. Although fossil echinoids are rarely found with the spines still attached, the detached spines are sometimes found in certain marine deposits of Cretaceous age. When the animal was alive these spines were used for locomotion and as protection from enemies.

Sea urchins, like all echinoderms are *gregarious*—that is, they commonly live together in large groups. Because of this, their remains are commonly found concentrated in relatively small areas where they occur in large numbers. Large "pockets" of fossil sea urchins are especially common in certain Cretaceous rocks.

Urasterella

Lovenechinus

Pentagonaster

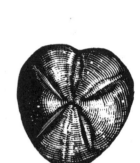

Hemiaster

Aganaster

Cidaris

Starfish

Echinoids

ANIMALS
WITH
BACKBONES

Although not commonly found by the average fossil-collector, the remains of the backboned creatures are from some of the most fascinating of all prehistoric animals. Among these are giant fishes, primitive amphibians, and an amazing variety of dinosaurs and other extinct reptiles. Included also are such unusual creatures as giant ground sloths, saber-toothed cats (or "tigers"), woolly mammoths, and huge flightless birds.

The chordates are the most advanced of all animals. They are characterized by the presence of a well-developed nervous system and a body supported by a *notochord* or *spinal column*. In some forms the internal supporting rod is composed of cartilage. In others it consists of bone.

Few of the lower chordates (subphylum Hemichordata) have left a fossil record. However, the members of class Graptolithina are an exception. The *graptolites* are a group of extinct colonial animals which were very abundant during early Paleozoic time.

They are characterized by a chitinous exoskeleton consisting of rows of cups or tubes which housed the living animal. These little "houses" were attached to single or branching stalks. Some of the stalks were anchored to the bottom and others grew on floats. Many of the floating forms were distributed over wide areas and thus are important as guide fossils. Graptolite remains are especially abundant in certain Ordovician and Silurian rocks.

Typically found in black shales, graptolites are usually preserved as carbon residues. These fossils somewhat resemble pen or pencil marks on the rocks and have been mistaken for Indian writing or hieroglyphics. Hence the name graptolites which literally means "written-stones." Graptolite remains are especially common in certain Ordovician and Silurian rocks.

Not all paleontologists agree as to exactly how these peculiar little creatures should be classified. In the past they have been assigned to the classes Hydrozoa, Scyphozoa, and Graptozoa of phylum Coelenterata. In addition, they were classified as bryozoans by certain of the early paleontologists. However, the latest scientific research indicates that the graptolites are some type of extinct hemichordate and we shall consider them as such.

The members of subphylum Vertebrata are the most advanced of all the chordates. They have a skull, a bony or cartilaginous *endoskeleton* (internal skeleton), with a vertebral column of bone or cartilage.

The vertebrates have been divided into two large groups called superclasses: the *Pisces* (fishes and their relatives) and *Tetrapoda* (the four-footed animals).

As mentioned earlier, the average amateur fossil hunter collects relatively few vertebrate remains. For this reason this group is not discussed in detail. We will, however, become acquainted with some typical vertebrates in order that you may have some understanding of this important group of animals.

Members of superclass Pisces, (Latin *piscis,* fish) are the simplest and most numerous of all vertebrates. They are aquatic, free-moving, and usually *cold-blooded* (their blood maintains the temperature of the surrounding water). Most breathe by means of *gills,* but some forms (the *lungfishes*) breathe by means of a lung developed from the air-bladder.

The *ostracoderms* (class *Ostracodermi*) are extinct, jawless fish related to the living lampreys and hagfishes. They first appeared in Ordovician time and were armored by a bony covering on the front part of their bodies. The ostracoderms are not only the earliest recorded fishes, they also appear to be the first backboned animals to inhabit our earth.

Another group of primitive armored fishes were the *placoderms* (class *Placodermi*). These fishes had jaws and were sharklike in appearance. One group, the *arthrodires,* were very heavily armored, had large powerful jaws, and grew to be as much as thirty feet in length.

Members of class *Chondrichthyes* have no air-bladder and no scales, the skeleton is composed of cartilage rather than bone. Represented by such familiar modern forms as the sharks and the rays, these fishes seem to have developed from the placoderms during Devonian time.

Shark's teeth are fairly common in many Cretaceous and Cenozoic formations. Most of them are in an excellent state of preservation and some are as much as ten inches long!

Class *Osteichthyes* includes the true bony fishes which are the most highly developed and abundant of all fishes. They have an internal bony skeleton, well-developed jaws, an air-bladder, and an outer covering of scales or bony plates. Typical examples are the trout, bass, perch, and cod.

Included also in this class are a primitive group of fish called *crossopterygians*. These were quite abundant during the Devonian and are believed to be the ancestors of the air-breathing amphibians. The modern *lungfishes* also belong to this class. Found now only in Australia, South America, and Africa, these creatures breathe by means of gills, as well as by primitive lungs which have been developed from the air-bladder. Although rare today, they were quite common during the Devonian period.

The remains of bony fishes have been collected from many different formations. Such fossils may be in the form of teeth, bones, scales, and an occasional well-preserved skeleton. Some very fine carbon impressions have also been found.

The four-footed animals (superclass Tetrapoda) are the most advanced animals. They are characterized by lungs, a three- or four-chambered heart,

Graptolites

Dendrograptus

Phyllograptus

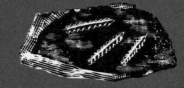

Diplograptus

Ostracoderm *Anglaspis*
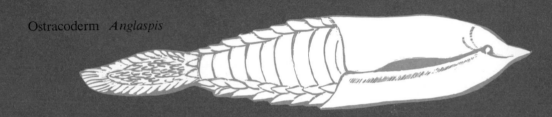

90

and paired appendages. Included here are the classes *Amphibia* (frogs, toads, and salamanders), *Reptilia* (lizards, snakes, turtles, and the extinct dinosaurs), *Aves* (birds), and *Mammalia* (including the mammals, such as men, dogs, whales, bats, etc.).

The earliest developed four-footed creatures were the *amphibians*. They are cold-blooded animals that breathe primarily by lungs and spend most of their life on land. But during their early stages of development they live in the water where they breathe by means of gills, as, for example, the tadpole stage of frogs.

The amphibians apparently developed from the crossopterygian fishes during late Devonian time. Because they were so abundant during the Mississippian, Pennsylvanian, and Permian periods, this part of geologic time is sometimes referred to as the "Age of Amphibians."

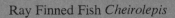
Ray Finned Fish *Cheirolepis*

Lobe Finned Fish *Osteolepis*

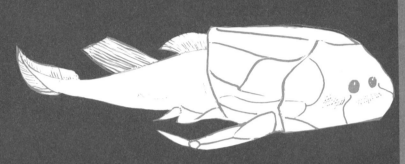

Placoderm *Bothriolepis*

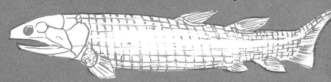

Shark *Pleuracanthus*

Lungfish *Scaumenacia*

Conodonts

(Believed to represent the teeth of some extinct fishes.)

One group of amphibians, the *labyrinthodonts,* or *stegocephalians,* may have been the ancestors of the reptiles.

Members of class Reptilia have become adapted to permanent life on land. They are cold-blooded and most have scaly skin. Reptiles have been much more abundant in the past than they are today, and they were of many different shapes and sizes.

Modern classifications recognize a large number of reptilian groups, but only the more important of these are mentioned below.

The *turtles* are reptiles in which the body is more or less completely enclosed by bony plates. Some of the Tertiary land tortoises were three to four feet long. One Cretaceous sea-going turtle, *Archelon,* grew to be as much as twelve feet long and weighed almost three tons!

Of particular interest among Permian vertebrates are the *pelycosaurs.* These mammal-like reptiles are normally characterized by a large fin- or sail-like structure on the back.

The *therapsids* were mammal-like reptiles that were well-adapted for life on land. Because they possessed both reptilian and mammalian characteristics, some scientists consider the therapsids to be a "missing link" between the reptiles and the mammals.

Among the more unusual reptiles of the Mesozoic were the "fish-lizards," or *ichthyosaurs.* These extinct, short-necked, marine reptiles resembled the modern dolphin or shark and some attained lengths of from 25 to 40 feet.

The *mosasaurs* were also sea-going reptiles. Some of these great reptiles grew to be as much as 50 feet long and their great gaping jaws were armed with a multitude of sharp, recurved teeth. They lived only during Cretaceous time.

Another group of interesting marine reptiles were the *plesiosaurs.* These peculiar creatures had a broad, turtle-like body, paddle-like flippers and a long neck and tail. Their rather unlikely appearance prompted one paleontologist to describe a long-necked plesiosaur as "resembling a snake pulled through a turtle shell!" Like the ichthyosaurs and the mosasaurs, plesiosaurs were abundant in Cretaceous seas.

The *phytosaurs,* or "plant-lizards" are rather poorly named, for the nature of their teeth clearly indicates that they were meat-eaters. The dominant reptiles of the Triassic period, these reptiles resembled crocodiles both in appearance and in their way of living. But this resemblance is only superficial, for the phytosaurs and the crocodiles represent two distinct groups of reptiles.

The *crocodiles* and *alligators* became adapted to the same type of habitat as that occupied by their forerunners, the phytosaurs. The early crocodilians were much larger than those of today. One such crocodile, *Phobosuchus,* represents the remains of the largest crocodile yet discovered. Its massive skull was six feet long and possessed exceptionally strong jaws. When living, this titanic beast probably had an overall length of almost 50 feet!

Some of the Mesozoic reptiles were able to fly. Known collectively as the *pterosaurs* ("wing-lizards"), the "flying dragons" were of many different shapes and sizes. Their batlike wings were supported by long, slender fingers and their bones were hollow. Their lightweight bodies and wide, skin-covered wings enabled them to soar or glide for great distances. The earliest pterosaurs were rather small and had a wingspread of about two feet. However, *Pteranodon,* a Cretaceous form, had a wingspread of more than twenty-seven feet.

Scientists have made some rather interesting speculations about the pterosaurs, or *pterodactyls,* as they are also called. It is believed, for instance, that their sight was excellent and that they had a good sense of balance. Their sense of smell, on the other hand, was poorly developed. The form of their brain, which is large for a reptile, indicated this. How can the brain of an extinct reptile be studied? By means of a *cast* of the brain cavity in the preserved skull. To prepare such a cast the brain cavity is filled with plaster of Paris or some other molding material. After the plaster hardens it is removed from the skull. The cast thus produced is a plaster replica of the soft brain which once filled the cavity. Such a cast can provide much information about the senses and intelligence of an animal.

The most spectacular and best-known prehistoric reptiles are the *dinosaurs.* The word "dinosaur" literally means "terrible-lizard." But not all dinosaurs were terrible and they actually were not even lizards! They do belong to the reptile class, however, and some of them were certainly among

Amphibian *Ichthyostega*

Reptile *Seymouria*

Reptile *Dimetrodon*

Reptile *Ichthyophis*

94

the largest and most terrible animals that ever walked the earth.

The dinosaurs are a distinctive group of reptiles that dominated Mesozoic life for well over 100 million years. In size, they ranged from as little as one foot to almost ninety feet in length, and from a few pounds to perhaps fifty tons in weight.

Some were carnivorous but the majority were *herbivorous* (plant-eaters). Some were *bipedal* (walked on their hind-legs), while others were *quadrupedal* (walked on all fours).

According to the structure of their hip bones, the dinosaurs have been separated into two great orders. These are the *Saurischia*, forms with a pelvic girdle like that of the lizard, and the *Ornithischia*, dinosaurs with a pelvic structure similar to that of the birds.

Saurischians were particularly abundant during the Jurassic and they had hip bones not unlike those of our modern lizards. These dinosaurs are

Marine reptile ichthyosaur

Flying reptile *Rhamporhynchus*

Reptile phytosaur skull

Reptile *Mystriosuchus*

divided into two rather specialized groups: the *theropods* (meat-eating, two-legged dinosaurs that varied greatly in size), and the *sauropods* (four-legged plant-eaters which were usually gigantic).

The *theropods* were saurischian dinosaurs that walked on birdlike hind legs. A long tail served to counterbalance the huge body. Most of them were flesh-eaters and some were among the most fearsome creatures that ever lived. These were the big-game hunters of their time—they can rightfully be compared with the lions and tigers of the present.

Ornitholestes, although not as large as some of the later carnivores, is typical of the early theropods and is one of the most interesting. A relatively small dinosaur, "Bird-Robber" was about six feet long. Its small, narrow skull was armed with sharp teeth, and rested on a rather long, flexible neck. The tail, as in all theropods, was relatively long and the birdlike hind legs were quite strong—well-adapted to running as well as for holding and tearing prey. The smaller front limbs bore three long, strong-clawed fingers.

Slightly built and fast-moving, *Ornitholestes* must have been an alert and able hunter. But whether we can accuse this so-called "Bird-Robber" of actually catching birds seems to be a debatable question. Many scientists believe that *Ornitholestes* could not have captured such game. It is more likely to have fed upon lizards and other small ground-dwelling animals of the time.

Tyrannosaurus rex literally means "King Tyrant Lizard." *Tyrannosaurus* appears to have ruled the dinosaur world; with his head standing almost 20 feet above the ground, this huge creature could have easily peered into the upper windows of a two-story house. *Tyrannosaurus* measured more than 47 feet from the tip of his great, tooth-studded skull to the end of his twenty-foot tail. When alive he must have weighed at least eight or ten tons. His short, thick neck was well designed to properly support his long, four-foot skull, and the cruel jaws were armed with sharp, double-edged teeth. These teeth, some of which were six-inches long and one-inch wide, were shaped like daggers.

Like all theropods, *Tyrannosaurus* walked on his powerful hind legs. His feet bore sharp, heavy claws. His two-clawed fore limbs, or arms, were so small that they were probably of rather limited use. The "Tyrant King" is indeed the ultimate in the development of flesh-eating dinosaurs.

The *sauropods* were the largest of all dinosaurs—some were almost ninety feet long and weighed as much as fifty tons. They are normally characterized by a long neck and tail with a rather short, stout body. They were all *quadrupedal;* that is, they walked on all fours. This is not surprising for such great weight could hardly have been supported by the hind limbs alone. When compared with the rest of the body, the sauropod skull was almost ridiculously small. This suggests that although the sauropods were among the largest creatures that ever lived, they were certainly *not* the most intelligent.

Unlike the meat-eating theropods, sauropods had weak jaws. Their teeth consisted basically of two kinds: round, peglike slightly pointed ones about the size of a pencil and those that were leaf-shaped or spoon-shaped. Both types of tooth structure indicate that the sauropods were herbivorous. They probably ate the tender water plants that grew in the swamps and marshes which these dinosaurs typically inhabited. The sauropods reached their maximum development and greatest size during late Jurassic time; it has thus been said that this period was the "Time of the Giants." After being introduced to such typical sauropods as *Brontosaurus* and *Diplodocus* you will most likely agree with that statement.

Brontosaurus literally means "Thunder Lizard." The man who named this dinosaur thought that *Brontosaurus* was so large that the earth must have certainly rumbled when he walked. Considering that the live weight of this huge creature might have been as much as 35 tons, this was not an unreasonable assumption!

The "Thunder Lizard's" massive, blimplike body was supported by four stocky legs. The hind legs were longer and stronger than the front ones and the broad padded feet were clawed. One massive, sharp, curved claw was present on each forefoot; each hind foot was provided with three similar claws. These may have been used to dig up plant material from the bottoms of streams and marshes. Although stout and thick, the brontosaur's leg joints were rather poorly constructed and held together by cartilage. This type of structure suggests that the *Brontosaurus* was not well-suited for walking on dry land. It has been suggested, therefore, that the "Thunder Lizard" spent most of his time wading about in shallow waters which would help support his great weight. Besides, *Brontosaurus* was probably much safer in the water than near the shore where certain of the great meat-eating dinosaurs were eagerly awaiting his appearance!

Brontosaurus had a long, strong tail which was quite thick where it joined the body. This whiplike tail might possibly have served as a weapon of defense in much the same manner that alligators and crocodiles use their tails today.

But most unusual of all was the tiny skull which was perched atop the long, snakelike neck. The small mouth contained rather weak, broad, spoon-shaped teeth which were confined to the front of the mouth. The brain cavity was extremely small; the organ which occupied it must have weighed less than one pound. The brain was so tiny in comparison to the rest of the body, that the "Thunder Lizard" most surely was not a "thinking" creature. Instead, it lived by instinct, knowing only to eat, sleep, lay eggs,

97

and escape its enemies. Although its mouth seems almost too small to have taken in enough food to keep this giant alive, the dinosaurs were reptiles and, like the cold-blooded, somewhat sluggish reptiles of today, probably required much less food than do warm-blooded animals.

Another familiar Jurassic giant is the dinosaur known as *Diplodocus*. Its name is derived from the Greek words for "double" and "beam"; it refers to the two projections which were located on the vertebrae of the animal.

Measuring more than 87 feet in length, *Diplodocus* is believed to have been the longest land-dwelling animal that ever lived. Although *Diplodocus* resembled *Brontosaurus*, its neck and tail were longer. In fact, approxi-

Dr. Brown, R. T. Bird, and Dr. Schaikjer
with the skull of Phobosuchus, *an extinct crocodile*
from the Cretaceous of Trans-Pecos Texas.
Photograph courtesy of the American Museum of Natural History.

mately one-third of its length was composed of the flexible S-shaped neck and more than half consisted of the long, tapered, whiplike tail. This left little room in between for the short 25-ton body.

The skull of *Diplodocus* was even smaller than that of the "Thunder Lizard" and its brain probably weighed only a few ounces. There were a number of rather blunt, weak, peglike teeth along the margin of the mouth.

Like the brontosaurs, *Diplodocus* spent much of his time in or near the water. This helped support his great weight and offered him some protection from the vicious meat-eating dinosaurs, that roamed the shore. As an added convenience to its water-dwelling existence, the nostrils of *Diplodocus* opened through a single hole placed well on the top of his head. The animal could thus breathe while most of the body was completely submerged.

The other order of dinosaurs, the Ornithischia, were herbivorous, bird-hipped reptiles. They were quite varied in form and size and appear to have been more highly developed than their lizard-hipped cousins.

Because they are so varied, dinosaur specialists have divided the bird-hipped dinosaurs into four suborders: the *Ornithopoda* (duck-billed dinosaurs), *Stegosauria* (plate-bearing dinosaurs), *Ankylosauria* (armored dinosaurs), and *Ceratopsia* (horned dinosaurs). Included among the "bird-hips" are some of the most peculiar animals that ever lived.

The ornithopods (the word means "bird-foot") were relatively large bipedal dinosaurs. They lived during Jurassic and Cretaceous times. Most members of this suborder are characterized by a more-or-less flattened, ducklike beak.

Probably the best-known ornithopod, or "duckbilled" dinosaur is *Anatosaurus*. The name is derived from the Greek words meaning "duck-lizard"; it describes well certain ducklike characteristics of this interesting animal. The most notable of these is the mouth of the animal which has been produced into a flat beak resembling that of a duck. In some dinosaur books *Anatosaurus* is referred to as *Trachodon*.

Apparently a common dinosaur in North America in late Cretaceous time, *Anatosaurus* walked on strong, three-toed feet. The feet were not clawed; rather, they were broad, rounded hoofs. The four-fingered forelimbs were shorter than the hindlimbs. The structure of the forelimbs suggests that

thecodonts

sauropods

ankylosaurs

stegosaurs

the "Duck Lizard" occasionally walked on four legs as well as two. It is also known that webs of skin were present between the fingers of *Anatosaurus* and similar webs may have been present on the feet. Structures of this type certainly would have been most useful to this water-loving reptile.

The thick, powerful tail was ideally constructed for swimming. It was probably used to propel the animal through the water by means of a side-to-side movement similar to that used by the present day crocodiles and alligators. On land, the tail apparently helped balance the animal when standing or walking.

The body of *Anatosaurus* was covered with rather thin, leathery, roughly pebbled skin, and there was a thin frill of skin running along the middle of the back from head to tail. This has been learned from a study of certain fossilized mummies in which the skin has been perfectly preserved.

The *stegosaurs,* or "plate-backed" dinosaurs, were among the most unusual bird-hipped dinosaurs. They had a very brief geologic history; they appeared first in Jurassic time and were apparently extinct by the early part of the Cretaceous period. Four-footed, plant-eating dinosaurs, the stegosaurs developed armor-plate and spikes to discourage attacks from the meat-eaters. Hence, the name *Stegosauria,* or "covered lizard."

The small-head, spiked tail, and plated back of *Stegosaurus* is prob-

100

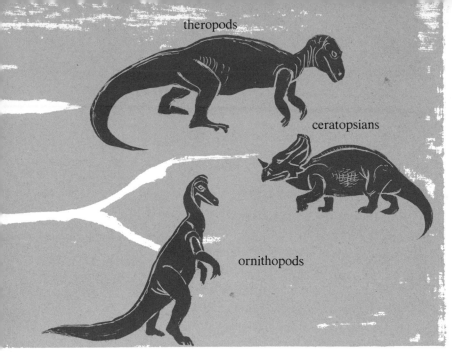

theropods

ceratopsians

ornithopods

ably already familiar to most of you. It is the most typical stegosaur and the one about which most is known.

Although actually a harmless plant-eater, *Stegosaurus* was a rather frightening creature to behold. It was about 20 feet long and stood almost nine feet high at the hips. The body was flattened from the sides and was supported by four stocky legs. Its front legs were considerably shorter than the rather long hind legs and this produced a strongly arched back. Although definitely quadrupedal, the nature of the hind legs suggests that *Stegosaurus'* ancestors must have walked erect. (As these dinosaurs became heavier, the hind limbs could not support their great weight and they eventually were forced to walk on all fours.)

Its small head was mounted on a rather short neck and was carried close to the ground. The teeth were weak and suited to chewing only soft vegetation. The size of the brain was no larger than a walnut; it probably weighed only about three ounces whereas the overall body weight ranged from seven to ten tons!

Perhaps you have heard it said that *Stegosaurus* had two brains, one in the head and one in the tail—this is not true. It is true, however, that this dinosaur had an enlargement of the spinal cord in the hip region. This mass of nervous tissue, approximately 20 times the size of the brain, served as a nerve center to control the tail and hind legs.

101

But the most characteristic feature of *Stegosaurus* was the double row of alternating bony plates which ran down the middle of the creature's back. These generally triangular plates were arranged vertically with the tips pointing upwards. The plates over the hips were as much as two feet tall and two and one-half feet wide at the base.

There were four large bony spikes located near the end of the tail of *Stegosaurus,* more than two feet long and five to six inches in diameter at their base. This heavily spiked tail must have been an effective protective weapon.

Although the stegosaurs disappeared during early Cretaceous time, this did not mark the end of the armored dinosaurs. The *ankylosaurs,* which lived during the Cretaceous period, were even more effectively armored than the plated forms which had preceded them.

Ankylosaurus was a dinosaur of moderate size (about 17 feet long and four feet high) with a broad, squat body protected by a heavy, shieldlike covering. Composed of heavy bony plates, this cover must have afforded considerable protection for this presumably slow-moving plant-eater. Its short, broad skull was also protected by bony armor-plate.

The ankylosaur body was supported by four short, stout limbs; it took strong legs to carry the heavy armament of this veritable "walking fortress." The tail, which was also heavily plated, ended in a great mass of bone. This massive natural "war club" must have effectively discouraged even the most persistent enemy of *Ankylosaurus*.

The *ceratopsians,* or horned dinosaurs, were the last major group of dinosaurs to appear. But before they disappeared they were present in large numbers and attained almost world-wide distribution in late Cretaceous time.

The word *Ceratopsia* means "horn face"; it refers to the fact that the typical ceratopsian had from one to three horns on its face. These dinosaurs walked on all four feet, and the body and tail were relatively short. The skull was typically long and massive and a bony frill protected the neck.

Triceratops, the three-horned ceratopsian, marks the high point in the development of this group. This large dinosaur was between 20 and 30 feet long and had an estimated weight of about ten tons. The neck and tail were short and the head was carried close to the ground. As is typical of most quadrupedal dinosaurs, the shoulders were low and the greatest height was at the hips.

The skull of *Triceratops* is unusually large and in some specimens they measure as much as eight feet in length—almost one-third the length of the body! The front of the skull and the jaws formed a hooked, parrotlike beak, and a long, sharp horn was located over each eye. A shorter, stouter horn stood upright on the nose.

The typical ceratopsian frill was a flaring, bony collar which extended back over the neck and shoulders like a hood. A skull structure of this type would provide considerable protection for the normally vulnerable neck region of the animal. The combination of sharp horns and heavy armor probably served *Triceratops* well, for it lived at the same time as *Tyrannosaurus* and other great Cretaceous meat-eating dinosaurs.

Another important group of backboned animals, the *birds,* made their appearance in Mesozoic time. Members of class Aves, birds are not commonly found as fossils because of the fragile nature of their skeletons. In spite of this, some interesting and important fossil birds have been discovered.

The earliest bird, *Archaeopteryx,* was found in Upper Jurassic rocks in Germany. Little more than a reptile with feathers, "Ancient-wing" was about the size of a crow, had a peculiar tail, and three claws on each wing. These unusual fossils furnish evidence of the close relationships between reptiles and birds, and they are among the most important fossils ever discovered.

The birds of Cretaceous time were more numerous and more specialized than those of the Jurassic. The structure of the skull, limbs, and bones was definitely more birdlike but many species still retained teeth.

Cenozoic birds closely resembled those of today. Although their fossils are relatively rare, they must have been almost as abundant and varied as the modern birds. Of particular interest are the giant flightless birds of the Tertiary. One such bird, *Dinornis* (meaning "terrible-bird"), stood ten to twelve feet tall and its eggs were almost a foot in diameter!

The members of class Mammalia are generally referred to as *mammals*. The best-known of all animals, mammals have a protective covering of hair,

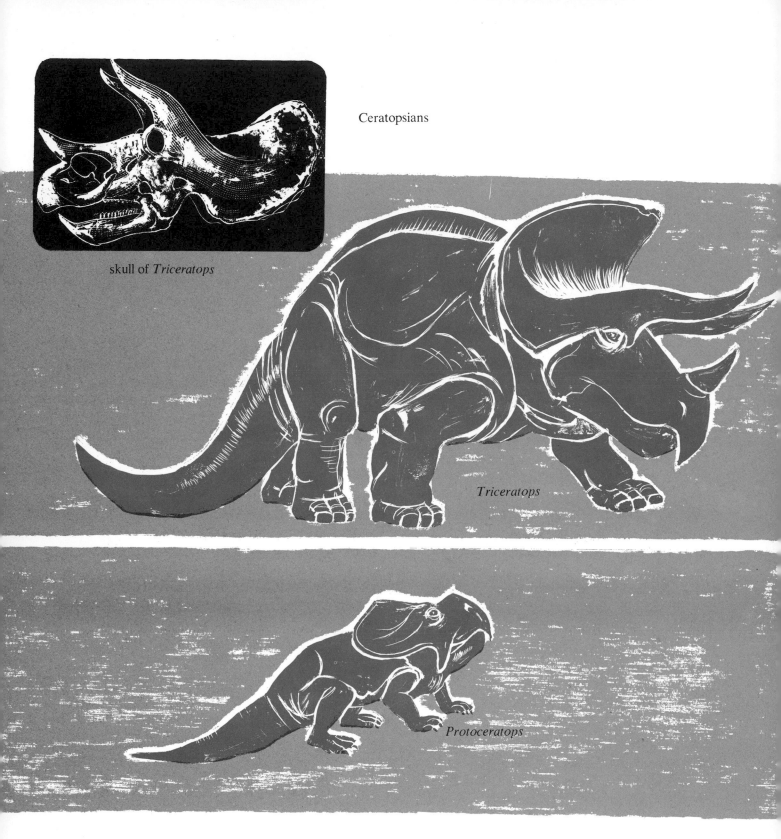

Ceratopsians

skull of *Triceratops*

Triceratops

Protoceratops

are warm-blooded, air-breathing, and nourish their young on milk.

Mammals first appeared in the Jurassic and were probably derived from mammal-like reptiles. Mammals were rare during Mesozoic time but multiplied and underwent many changes during the Cenozoic. Some Cenozoic mammals grew to be very large and assumed unusual shapes as had the dinosaurs which had gone before them. Although most of these peculiar creatures were doomed to early extinction, they are well known from their fossils.

Recent classifications of the mammals recognizes several subclasses and numerous orders and suborders. Our discussion here, however, must be brief and no attempt at detailed classification is made. We will, nevertheless, become acquainted with some of the more unusual Cenozoic mammals in this chapter.

Modern mammals can be placed in three major groups: the monotremes, the marsupials, and the placentals.

Monotremes are primitive mammals that lay eggs. These peculiar creatures are represented by the duck-billed platypus and the spiny anteater, both of which live in Australia and New Guinea. Although they have a short geologic history, these animals are of considerable evolutionary significance. They probably developed from some of the early mammal-like reptiles.

The *marsupials* are pouched animals like the oppossum and kangaroo. In this group the young are born in a very immature state and then crawl into a pouch on the mother's belly. They remain there until large enough to "go out on their own." Most of the marsupials (for example, wombats and kangaroos) inhabit Australia, but oppossums live in both North and South America.

The most abundant land mammals are the *placentals*. Unlike the marsupials, placental animals undergo considerable development before they are born. At birth they typically resemble the fully developed adult animal and are well adapted to independent existence.

The placental animals are known as *therians*, because they belong to the mammalian subclass *Theria*. This subclass has been divided into several orders, but only the more important ones are discussed here.

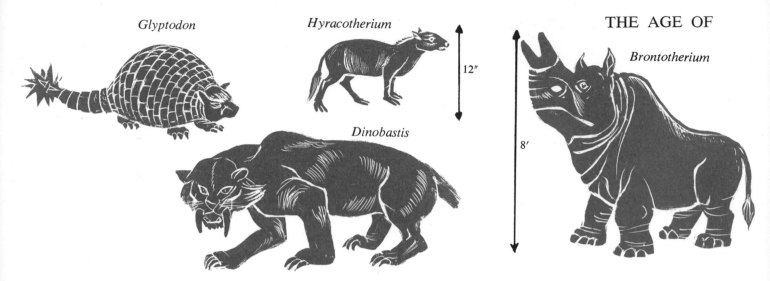

Glyptodon Hyracotherium 12" Dinobastis THE AGE OF Brontotherium 8'

Members of the order *Edentata* are a rather primitive group of mammals represented by such living forms as the anteaters, tree sloths, and armadillos. Members of this group were common in the southern part of the United States in Pleistocene and Pliocene time. One such form was *Mylodon,* one of the extinct giant ground sloths. These huge sloths were quite heavy and some of them stood as much as 15 feet tall. These great creatures were the forerunners of the modern tree sloths of South America.

Another interesting representative of this order was the *glyptodont.* These peculiar mammals, which were ancestral to the present-day armadillos, developed at about the same time as the ground sloths. *Glyptodon* is quite characteristic of this group. This armadillo-like beast had a solid turtle-like shell that in some forms was as much as four feet high. From the front of the bone-capped head to the tip of its tail, a large individual might be as much as 15 feet long. The thick heavy tail was protected by a series of bony rings, and in some species the end of the tail was developed into a bony heavily spiked club.

The meat-eating animals belong to the order *Carnivora.* Such animals are called carnivores and are characterized by clawed feet and by teeth which are adapted for tearing and cutting flesh. They were first represented by an ancient group of animals called *creodonts,* and this short-lived group first appeared in the Paleocene and were extinct by the end of the Eocene. They ranged from the size of a weasel to that of a large bear, and their claws were sharp and well developed. Their teeth, however, were not so specialized as those of modern carnivores, and the creodont brain was relatively small. It is assumed that these animals had a very low order of intelligence when compared to the more advanced carnivores of today.

106

Uintatherium

Woolly rhinocerous

These early meat-eaters were followed by more specialized carnivores which developed throughout Cenozoic time. Some examples of these are the saber-toothed cat, *Smilodon,* and the dire wolf, *Canis dirus.*

The order *Dinocerata* consists of an extinct group of gigantic mammals commonly called *uintatheres. Uintatherium,* which is typical of the group, had three pairs of blunt horns, and the males had dagger-like upper tusks. Some of the uintatheres were as large as a small elephant and stood as much as seven feet tall at the shoulders. The size of the brain in relation to the size of the body suggests that these animals were not so intelligent as most mammals. Uintatheres are known from rocks ranging from Paleocene to Eocene in age.

Members of the order *Proboscidea,* the elephants and their relatives, first appeared in the late Eocene of Africa. They were about the size of a small modern elephant but had larger heads and shorter trunks. Proboscidean development is marked by an increase in size, change in skull and tooth structure, and elongation of the trunk. Two well-known fossil proboscideans are the *mammoth* and the *mastodon.* The mastodons resembled the elephants, but the structure of their teeth was quite different. Moreover, the mastodon skull was lower than that of the elephant and the tusks were exceptionally large—some reaching a length of nine feet.

There were several types of mammoths, and the *woolly mammoth* is probably the best known. This animal lived until the end of the Pleistocene and, like the woolly rhinoceros discussed below, is known from ancient cave paintings and frozen remains. Information gathered from these sources indicates that this great beast had a long coat of black hair with a woolly undercoat.

107

marine carnivores

creodonts

bear

dog family

raccoon family

fissipedes

weasel family

civets

hyenas

CARNIVORE FAMILY TREE

cat family

pigs and peccaries

hippopotamus

camel

deer

giant hogs

pig group

primitive ruminants

giraffes

chevrotains

prongbucks

cattle family

ARTIODACTYL FAMILY TREE (even-toed mammals)

During the Pleistocene, mammoths were widespread over the United States, and their remains are abundant in many stream deposits of this age. Such fossils are commonly found in certain sand and gravel pits.

The order *Perissodactyla,* or odd-toed animals, are a group of mammals in which the central toe on each limb is greatly enlarged. Modern representatives include the horses, rhinoceroses, and tapirs. Extinct members of the Perissodactyla include the *titanotheres* and *baluchitheres,* all of which grew to tremendous size and took on many unusual body forms.

One of the first perissodactyls was *Hyracotherium* (also called *Eohippus*), which is the earliest known horse. This small animal was about a foot high and his teeth indicate a diet of soft food. Following the first horse, there is a long series of fossil horses which provide much valuable information on the history of this important group of animals.

The *titanotheres* appeared first in the Eocene when they were about the size of a sheep. By middle Oligocene time they had increased to gigantic proportions but still had a small and primitive brain. *Brontotherium* was slightly rhinoceroslike in appearance and is believed to be the largest land animal that ever inhabited the North American continent. This animal was about eight feet tall at the shoulders; a large bony growth protruded from the skull and this was extended into a flattened horn, which was divided at the top.

The rhinoceroses are also odd-toed animals, and there are many interesting and well-known fossils in this group. The *woolly rhinoceros* was a Pleistocene two-horned form that ranged from southern France to northeastern Siberia. The woolly rhinoceros is well known from complete carcasses recovered from the frozen tundra of Siberia and from remains that were found preserved in an oil seep in Poland. These unusual specimens plus cave paintings made by early man have given a complete and accurate record of this creature.

Baluchitherium, the largest land mammal known to science, was a hornless rhinoceros that lived in late Oligocene and early Miocene time. This immense creature measured approximately 25 feet from head to tail, stood almost 18 feet high at the shoulder. It must have weighed many tons. Remains of these creatures have not been discovered in North America, and they appear to have been restricted to Central Asia.

The mammals assigned to order *Artiodactyla* are the even-toed hoofed mammals and include such familiar forms as pigs, camels, deer, goats, sheep, and hippopotamuses. This is a large and varied group of animals, but the basic anatomical structure of the limbs and teeth show well the relationship between the different forms. Artiodactyls are abundant fossils in rocks ranging from Eocene to Pleistocene in age.

Among the more interesting artiodactyls are the *entelodonts,* giant swine-like creatures that lived during Oligocene and early Miocene time. They were distinguished by a long, heavy skull that held a relatively small brain. The face was marked by large knobs which were located beneath the eyes and on the underside of the lower jaw. Although these knoblike structures were blunt, they had the appearance of short horns. Certain of these giant swine attained a height of six feet at the shoulders and had skulls that measured three feet in length.

Another important group of even-toed animals are the camels. The first known camels have been reported from rocks of upper Eocene age, and these small forms underwent considerable specialization of teeth and limbs as they developed in size. Many of the camels that lived during the middle Cenozoic had long legs which were well adapted to running and long necks which would have allowed the animals to browse on the leaves of tall trees. These early forms eventually underwent more specialization until they reached their present state of development.

Thus ends our parade of plants and animals, both old and new, that we have actually only briefly scanned. Many groups of organisms could not be mentioned for there are too many of them.

It is hoped, however, that these chapters have given you a greater appreciation of the wonderful world of nature and of the plants and animals of days gone by. In the next chapter we will learn how the earth scientist has used their remains in reconstructing the history of the earth.

Zinjanthropus skull: over 600,000 years old

READING
THE
RECORD

About 250 million years ago much of North America was covered by great swampy forests. One of the largest of these forests was located in what is now the state of Illinois. Suppose that we take an imaginery Sunday afternoon stroll through this prehistoric swampland forest.

Do not expect to pick any wildflowers as we walk through the woods, for this is the Pennsylvanian period and the flowering plants have not yet appeared on earth. Nor will we do any bird-watching. The first bird will not appear until the Jurassic period—some 50 or 60 million years from now! But we will see so many other interesting sights that the birds and flowers will hardly be missed.

Entering this great gloomy forest is almost like entering another world. The trees, for example, are quite unlike those of today and the typical forest-dwelling animals are nowhere to be seen. The forest is dominated by the peculiar scale trees. Some of them are six feet in diameter and tower more than 100 feet above the woodland floor. Their bark is marked by peculiar diamond-shaped leaf scars which give their trunks a scalelike appearance. The leaves, arranged in a spiral around the trunk and branches, resemble great pine needles.

Underfoot, the moist forest floor is carpeted by a luxuriant growth of mosses, ferns, and other moisture-loving plants. These thrive in the damp, warm climate of Pennsylvanian time. Beneath this living carpet of green, lies a dense mat of rotting leaves, logs, and animal matter.

As we move along the trail, insects run over the ground, up the trunks of trees, and dart swiftly through the air. These, too, remind one of life on another planet. There are giant may flies, eight-inch cockroaches, and dragonflies with 30-inch wingspreads!

Here and there may be seen open pools of dark, murky water. Hiding among the rushes which line their banks are numerous amphibians, relatives of our modern frogs and toads. Luckily, we need not worry about snakes. The only reptiles present are small lizard-like forms about one foot long. It will be many millions of years before the first snake will slither across the earth's surface. We must, nevertheless, step with caution. Many large spiders, scorpions, and centipedes live among the dank decaying vegetation on the forest floor.

Maybe you are thinking of fishing in one of these pools. Fish you may, but do not expect to catch such familiar forms as trout, perch, or bass. Instead, be prepared to hook strange, armor-plated fishes with big, thick scales or strange eel-like amphibians. With a bit of luck you might even land a lungfish—a peculiar creature that has both gills and lungs. Its fins, which look somewhat like legs, are often used to help this fish crawl about on land!

Although our Sunday afternoon stroll was purely imaginary, the swampy forests, giant insects, and "walking" fish of Pennsylvanian time were not. How do we know? The proof of their existence is recorded in the rocks. Fortunately, the remains of scale trees, ferns, and many other plants are faithfully preserved in the great coal deposits of Illinois. There is also proof that giant insects lived in this forest. Imprints of their bodies are commonly found in the clays, shales, and limestones deposited during Pennsylvanian time.

Diatoms

Neuropteris

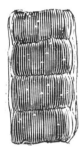

Calamites

Lepidodendron

Sigillaria

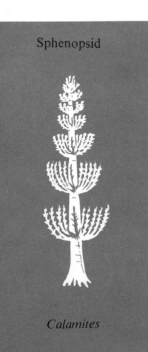

Sphenopsid

Lycopods

Gymnosperms

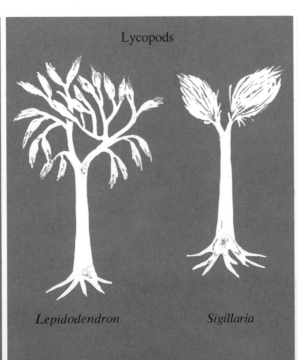

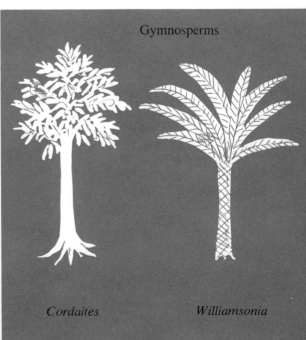

Calamites

Lepidodendron

Sigillaria

Cordaites

Williamsonia

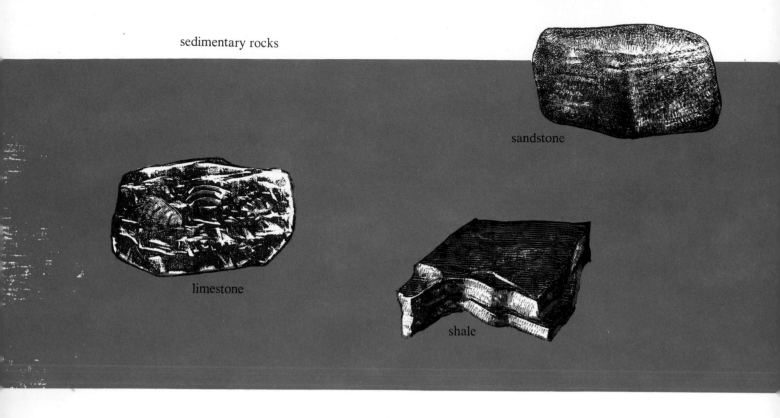

sedimentary rocks

sandstone

limestone

shale

The record in the rocks is read by studying the rocky layers of the earth as one might study a giant history book. There, in the stony "pages" of the earth's crust, are found the tracks, trails, bones, and stones which tell the fascinating story of life long ago.

The geologic story begins with the oldest rocks that are known. These rocks, because they were formed first, are normally found deeply buried beneath younger or newer rocks. Thus, earth history is read from the bottom up. The earliest formed rock layers correspond to the first pages in our giant history book. Later chapters are found in the younger rocks which are located nearer the surface.

Unfortunately, rock layers are not always found in the same sequence in which they were originally deposited. In times past, earthquakes and other great disturbances within the crust have caused many rock "pages" to become shuffled and out of place—some have even been lost. This makes the story more difficult to read and the scientist must then turn detective and search for clues that will make it possible to "fill in the blanks."

The most valuable clues in solving these puzzles in earth history are marine *sedimentary rocks*. These rocks were formed when salt-water sedi-

116

rock with mud cracks

rock with ripple marks

ments, such as limy muds, sands, or shell beds, were compressed and cemented together to form rocks. This type of rock commonly contains the fossilized remains of the organisms which inhabited prehistoric seas and these fossils may provide much information about the rocks in which they are found.

Igneous and *metamorphic* rocks, on the other hand, rarely contain traces of life. The igneous rocks were once hot and molten and had no life associated with them. Metamorphic rocks have been so greatly changed or distorted that any fossils that were present in the original rock have usually been destroyed or so altered as to be unrecognizable.

Although they do not normally tell us much about ancient plants and animals, igneous and metamorphic rocks do provide other types of geologic information. For example, great lava fields are mute evidence of periods of volcanic activity. Likewise, highly distorted metamorphic rocks normally indicate periods of violent disturbance and upheaval in the earth's crust. Some of these earth movements have been so severe that limestone, a typical sedimentary rock, has been transformed into marble, a metamorphic rock.

117

In 1795, a young surveyor named William Smith was asked to plan the route of a new canal that was to be dug in southern England. Knowing that the type of rock through which the canal would be dug would have a direct bearing on the cost of the project, Smith needed to know something of the geology of the area concerned. There were few trained geologists in those days, so the young engineer had to make his own geological studies. Luckily for Smith, however, his hobby was collecting rocks and fossils—a pastime which he soon put to practical use in the field.

In digging through the different rock formations, Smith learned that the various rock strata could be identified by the fossils they contained. He noticed also that the fossils found in each rock formation were different from those in the rocks above and below it. Recognizing fossils to be useful field guides, Smith was soon able to predict the location and physical characteristics of rocks below the surface by means of the fossils he found exposed in canals and quarries. Known today as *correlation*, Smith's technique of "matching" the rocks and fossils from different areas is one of the most important processes used in deciphering earth history. As a result of his work, "Strata" Smith, as he was later nicknamed, constructed the first geologic map of England, Wales, and part of Scotland.

We see, then, that fossils are among the more important clues in piecing together the puzzles of earth history. These relics of ancient life are helpful because each specimen usually tells something about when it lived, where it lived, and how it lived.

For instance, one question that is always of interest is *when* did a certain fossil live? If this is known, it may provide important information about the age of the rocks in which it is found. This is possible because certain plants and animals lived only a short time in geologic history but were rather widely distributed during their relatively short life. Some of these remains are so characteristic of certain strata that they have been called *guide,* or *index fossils*. Such fossils are particularly helpful in correlation because they are normally associated only with rocks of one certain age. Guide fossils that are easy to identify and likely to be found in great numbers are especially useful in correlation.

Jurassic

Triassic

Permian

Carboniferous

Devonian

Silurian

Ordovician

Cambrian

Precambrian

Grand Canyon rock strata

Why is it desirable to know *where* an organism lived? We know, of course, that most plants live on the land. It is reasonably safe to assume, then, that the rocks which contain plant fossils were probaby formed on land. It is also known that certain kinds of animals live only in sea water. Thus, if we find fossilized sea animals in a rock this indicates that the rock was probably formed at the bottom of an ancient sea, and what is now dry land was once covered by water. By comparing the distribution of marine fossils to the distribution of land-dwelling forms, one can draw maps of different regions to show the geography of these areas as it might have been at various times in the geologic past. Maps of this type are called *paleogeographic* (literally "ancient geographic") *maps,* and show the location of ancient seas and land masses. Knowing where fossils lived makes possible the construction of accurate paleogeographic maps.

Not too long ago a scientific expedition discovered the remains of fossil ferns in Antarctica. Another group of scientists found fossilized magnolias in Greenland. Unusual discoveries of this type permit fossils to tell yet another story. They tell us that the climates of these regions were much warmer than they are today. Likewise, coal deposits commonly contain the remains of ferns and other plants which suggest warm, swampy conditions. Yet, many of these coal deposits are found in parts of the world that are much too cold and dry to support this type of vegetation today.

But the most important and interesting tale told by fossils is the story of the development of life on earth. The story begins, of course, in the older rocks. Fossils found in these rocks are usually primitive and relatively simple. However, a study of similar specimens that lived in later geologic time shows that these fossils become progressively more advanced and complex in the younger rocks. Thus, as we trace their development throughout geologic history, it is possible to learn when these organisms lived and how they have progressed and changed.

Fossils also have practical value. Many important mineral resources are known to occur in fossiliferous rocks. When this happens the geologist uses the fossils as clues in the search for geologic formations which contain valuable deposits of ore, coal, oil, and natural gas.

Some fossils are used for this purpose even though they are buried miles beneath the earth's surface! These are the tiny microfossils that are used by the oil geologist. Because they are very small, they are not likely to be broken by the drill bit while drilling for oil. They can be brought to the surface without damage to their original structure.

To study these fossils from deep within the earth, the micropaleontologist washes the well cuttings which have been taken from the bore hole of the well. The microfossils are separated from the surrounding rock fragments, mounted on special slides, and then studied under the microscope. Fossils obtained in this way serve as markers which help tell the geologist something about the deeply buried rocks that are being drilled and may lead to the discovery of oil.

121

Psilophyton

LET'S GO FOSSIL HUNTING

Hunting for fossils can be a most exciting adventure. As you search through a quarry or along the side of a hill, you are on the trail of once-living creatures that are often more strange than any animals that are living today. Here is a hobby that not only provides opportunity for exercise and relaxation in the great outdoors, but also makes possible enjoyable inside work, cleaning and identifying individual specimens. Along with this the fossil hunter can broaden his knowledge of the earth, its rocks, and of life long ago.

Whether you find the tooth of a shark or the shell of a snail, you will experience a great thrill when you make your first fossil discovery. At first you may find it difficult to believe that the rocks you are standing on represent the bottom of some prehistoric sea and that the fossil you have picked up once lived in those long-vanished waters. But as you collect more fossils and gain more experience you will begin to think of fossils as the paleontologist does—not as inanimate rocks, but as living animals.

From Geology Department,
Lamar State College of Technology,
Beaumont, Texas.

124

It is not only fun to collect fossils, it is also inexpensive. One does not need the elaborate materials and costly equipment required by some hobbies. But as in any "collecting" hobby a certain amount of basic "know-how" is helpful. Consequently, the successful "rockhound" knows where to look, what equipment to use, and the most effective methods of collecting.

Fossil-collecting requires a minimum amount of supplies and equipment. Fortunately, this material is inexpensive and most fossil-collecting equipment can be found in the household of the average family.

The basic tool in the fossil-collector's kit is the *hammer*. At first you can probably borrow a hammer from home. Later, as you become more experienced, you will probably want to get a *geological hammer*. These hammers, also called *mineralogist's* or *prospector's picks,* are of two types. One type has a square head on one end and a pick on the other. The second type is similar to a stonemason's or bricklayer's hammer and has a chisel end instead

From Geology Department,
Lamar State College of Technology,
Beaumont, Texas.

of the pointed pick end. You will find that the square head is useful in break-ing or chipping harder rocks. The pick or chisel end can be used for digging, prying, and splitting soft rocks.

Of course, you will need a *collecting bag* in which to carry your equip-ment, fossils, and other supplies. Look around the house and you will prob-ably find a Boy Scout knapsack, hunting bag, or some other suitable bag.

Sometimes fossils are hard to free from the surrounding rocks. A good steel *chisel* is just the thing for removing these stubborn specimens from their stony tombs. Get both ½- and 1-inch widths and you can handle most any specimen that you are likely to find. A small *punch* or *awl* is handy for removing small or fragile specimens from the softer rocks.

Many fine specimens that have been carefully collected in the field have been broken on the trip back home. To avoid such a mishap it is advisable to carry along sufficient *wrapping materials*. Each fossil should be wrapped carefully as it is collected. The more fragile specimens may be wrapped in cotton or tissue paper. Small match boxes or plastic pill vials filled with cotton will protect even the most delicate fossils. One more precaution: Always place the heavier specimens on the bottom of the bag and the lighter fossils on top.

Small *paper labels* (about two by three inches) are handy to have along. Data such as the collector's name, collecting locality, date of collection, and the geologic formation should be recorded on these. Labels may be cut from wrapping paper, index cards, or a small scratch pad. A properly completed label should be placed inside each bag of fossils from the locality described on the label.

Paper or cloth bags can be used to separate specimens from different collecting localities. Use heavy-duty hardware bags for rough, heavy specimens; medium-weight grocery bags are satisfactory for smaller fossils. Collecting locality data may be written on the side of the bag or on a label placed inside with the fossils. As an added precaution, many collectors do both. The advanced collector may want to use a cloth geological sample bag like that used by the professional geologist. This type of bag has an opening equipped with a drawstring and a cloth-backed label sewn along one side. They may be purchased from geological supply houses.

Last, but by no means least, the collector should never be without a *pencil, notebook,* and some type of *map.* All too often, important specimens are found to be useless because the locality where the fossil was collected is not known. *Never* rely on memory. Instead, carefully and accurately record all that is known about the location where the fossil was found. A small pocket notebook is inexpensive and just right to carry in the field.

Use a highway or county map to find the geographic location of each collecting locality. Such maps are usually available for each county of the state and can probably be obtained from your state highway department.

Helpful, but not necessary, are the following: (1) a *magnifying glass* (about 10 power) for looking at smaller specimens: (2) a *compass* for more accurate location of collecting localities; (3) *adhesive* or *masking tape*— locality information can be written on the tape and applied directly to the fossil; and (4) a *fossil guide* if one is available for your state. (Write the

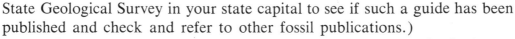

Basic kinds of rocks
in the United States

igneous rocks

metamorphic rocks

sedimentary rocks

127

State Geological Survey in your state capital to see if such a guide has been published and check and refer to other fossil publications.)

Before starting on a fossil-collecting trip it is wise to do a bit of advance planning. If you have some idea of where you are going and what you are looking for, your chances for good hunting will be greatly increased.

If at all possible take your first trip with an experienced collector or an organized group such as a museum class or rock and mineral club. With proper guidance you will soon learn to recognize the type of locality where fossils are most likely to be found. You will also become familiar with the fundamentals of field-collecting.

Where does one look for fossils? This is one of the first things that you must learn. As mentioned earlier, igneous and metamorphic rocks are not likely to contain fossils. Avoid rocks of this type and look instead for marine sedimentary rocks. These rocks were deposited under conditions that were favorable for organisms during life and which made possible their preservation after death. Limestones, limy shales, marls, and certain types of sandstones are typically deposited under such conditions.

Look especially for places where rocks formed from salt-water sediments lie relatively flat and have not been greatly disturbed by heat, pressure, and other, physical or chemical changes. If the rocks have been excessively folded or fractured, there is great likelihood that any fossils that were present have been damaged or destroyed by this action.

One of the best places to collect fossils is in a quarry. Rock exposures in quarries are relatively fresh but have usually undergone enough weathering to free some of the fossils. In a limestone quarry look carefully in the marl or shale layers that may separate the thicker and harder beds of limestone. Sand and gravel quarries are also good places to look. Petrified wood and the bones of mammals such as mammoths, mastodons, horses, and camels are known to occur in many sand and gravel pits.

Before collecting in a quarry (or any other private property) be sure to obtain the permission of the owners. The superintendent or foreman will often direct you to the best collecting places. More important, however, he can warn you of any blasting or other dangerous operations that may take place while you are in the quarry. Needless to say, you should keep away from trucks and machinery and stay out of the way of the workmen. If you follow these simple rules, you, and other collectors, will be welcome to return again.

Pay particular attention to all highway and railroad cuts. Rocks exposed in these places are usually still in their original position and are fairly well weathered. Cuts made by recent construction are usually more productive after they have undergone a period of weathering. This helps to separate the fossils from their surrounding rocks.

Canyons, gullies, and stream beds are often good hunting grounds. These areas are continuously being eroded by weathering and stream action, and new material is uncovered year after year.

Sometimes you may find fossils in freshly plowed fields, especially if there is fossiliferous bedrock beneath the surface. Incidentally, Indian relics may also be found in this way.

If you live in an area where there are abandoned coal mines, check the dumps of waste rock around the mine shafts. Many fine specimens of well-preserved plant fossils have been found at such places.

Along certain parts of the Atlantic and Pacific coasts, beachcombing may pay off. This is especially true of certain stretches of beach in New Jersey, Massachusetts, Delaware, Florida, Maryland, Oregon, and Washington. Both vertebrate and invertebrate remains have been found at some of these localities.

Once you have found a likely collecting spot, you should examine the ground very carefully. Get down on your hands and knees or sit down if possible. Take your time in one spot before moving—many of the fossils you pick up have probably been passed over by some hasty or impatient collector. Keep your eyes peeled for pieces of rock bearing shell fragments, leaf imprints, or other traces of plant or animal remains. These are the clues that may lead you to larger and more complete specimens.

129

*Typical
crinoidal
limestone*

If the fossils have been freed by weathering, they can simply be picked up and put in the collecting bag. If not, carefully chip away the surrounding rock or loosen it with your chisel. Take your time when chiseling. The best way to do this is to chisel a narrow trough around the fossil. Be sure to always point the chisel *away* from the specimen. When the trough is as deep, or deeper, than the fossil, chisel beneath the pedestal that the fossil is resting on and the specimen should break free. Don't take a chance on ruining a good specimen by trimming it too closely in the field. Final cleaning and preparation of fossils is best done at home.

Before you leave a collecting locality be sure that you have recorded its geographic location and the geologic age of the rock in which the fossils were found. The place should be located on the map and the locality data (name of county, state, highway number, etc.) should be entered in the notebook. Enter this information as clearly as possible so that you, or another collector, could easily return to the site for additional collecting.

If a county map is available, mark the locality directly on the map. You should then write the locality data on a label and drop it in the bag of fossils collected at that particular locality. It is wise to keep specimens from different localities in individual cloth or paper bags and make every attempt to keep the labels with their respective fossils. Always remember that *a fossil without a locality is hardly worth the paper it is wrapped in.*

Most of the areas in which you will be collecting will be on private property. Always ask the owner's permission before entering and tell him what you are looking for.

Consider yourself to be a guest of the property owner. Respect his livestock, fences, and other property, and leave the area cleaner than it was when you entered. Above all, close any gates that you have opened and be particularly careful of fire. If these precautions and simple courtesies are followed, future collectors will most likely be welcome to return for additional collecting.

For your own sake, and the sake of fellow collectors who may be with you, always be careful in the field. When collecting along the face of a quarry or cliff, be particularly careful not to dislodge rocks or boulders that may fall on someone below you. Be cautious when working at the bottom of a cliff lest you disturb loose rocks which might fall on you.

Use your hammer cautiously. Do not hammer in such a way that flying rock fragments will hit you or your companions. If it becomes necessary to do a lot of hammering and chiseling, it is a good idea to wear safety goggles to protect your eyes.

Once you have learned these simple "hows" and "wheres" of fossil hunting you will be well on your way to enjoying one of America's fastest growing hobbies.

From Geology Department,
Lamar State College of Technology,
Beaumont, Texas.

WHAT FOSSIL IS IT?

When you are a "pebble-pup," or beginning collector, you will probably be content to know if your specimen is an oyster or a snail, or a fern or a bone. But once you become a full-fledged rockhound, you will want to know the scientific name of each specimen.

Although fossil identification may seem somewhat confusing at first, you will soon learn that it is one of the more interesting and enjoyable aspects of fossil collecting. Then, too, if you are going to display your fossils you certainly need to know what to call them! In fact, the first step in establishing a worthwhile fossil collection is to show only those fossils that are properly identified by their scientific name and geologic age.

When you first begin to identify fossils, it may be helpful to show them to a geology teacher if there is a college or university nearby. Most teachers are glad to help and will probably have similar specimens in their own collections. In addition, many public school science teachers are familiar

Photograph by section of photography,
Chicago Natural History Museum.

with fossils and can offer helpful suggestions as to how to classify your material.

Museums of natural history are also good places to get assistance. If the museum has a geological collection, maybe they will let you compare your specimens with the fossils in their collections. Try to determine whether any of the museum's fossils came from the same general area in which yours were found. You may want to ask some of the museum employees for advice. They may be able to tell you where you should start looking in the collections and thus save you time.

If there are practicing professional geologists in your city, they are also usually glad to help the amateur. These men are normally familiar with the geology of the local area and can suggest publications which can be used to identify your specimens. Refer to the "yellow pages" of your telephone directory to see if there are any geologists in your city. They may be employed by an oil or mining company or as consulting geologists, in business for themselves.

Many times local librarians can recommend books, encyclopedias, or other publications that will be of help. And do not overlook help from members of a local rock or mineral club, if one is available. Many times more experienced collectors can pass along good ideas and tell you exactly which books to consult.

Some fossils, especially the more common ones, will be relatively easy to identify. Others will be more difficult and you may have to look in many books, journals, and other publications dealing with fossils.

Once you have located publications that appear to be related to your material, the fossils in question should be closely compared with any illustrations that are shown. If you find photographs or drawings similar to the specimens that you have collected, examine them closely. Next, carefully look at your fossils and note their more characteristic features. Then, compare them again with the illustrations and descriptions in the book.

It is usually best to try first to determine the phylum or class to which the specimen belongs. For example, although we may not know the genus and species of a certain fossil, we do know that it looks like a snail. So we call it a gastropod (for class Gastropoda, the snail class). This is, at least,

Cretaceous cephalopod *Turrilites*   Pennsylvanian gastropod *Worthenia*

a start in determining the scientific name. The fossil snail in question may also possess definite features which suggest that it should be placed in a certain order or family. Once this has been determined, a careful comparison of the fossil with the reference material will probably lead you to the genus and species.

The illustrations and descriptions in this book should help you to identify some of the more common invertebrate fossils. But the book was not designed primarily as a fossil identification guide, so other publications should be consulted as well.

It may also be helpful to know the common name of the fossil. However, some fossils have more than one common name, so it is better to learn the scientific name and avoid confusion.

In addition to the above sources of information, you may want to consult your state geological survey. Most states have bureaus of this sort which are concerned with geologic research. If it is convenient, you may wish to show your fossils to one of the state geologists and ask his help in classifying your fossils. If not, you may want to write your state survey for information on the fossils in your area. Some states have published "popular" or non-technical books on fossils and fossil-collecting. These are designed especially for the amateur collector.

HOW TO CARE FOR YOUR FOSSILS

A good collector, the full-fledged fossil-hunter, wants to show off his fossils to anyone who will look at them. He knows that sharing his collection with others is one of the most enjoyable aspects of this fascinating hobby.

He also has learned that fossils require a certain amount of attention before they are ready to show off. The first thing, of course, is to clean them. Next, each fossil should be provided with a label that tells what it is and where it was collected. Finally, each specimen should be displayed in the most interesting and attractive manner possible. Any fossil collector can start his own museum of earth history.

Although it may sometimes be advisable to do some preliminary cleaning of fossils in the field, this should be done only when necessary. The final cleaning and preparation of fossils is best done at home where sufficient time and the proper materials are available.

Before starting the final cleaning, it will be helpful to place the fossils in water and let them soak overnight. And, by the way, be sure to keep track of the identifying label that you placed in each sack as you collected. It is a good idea to place this under or alongside the container the fossils are soaking in.

Some rocks are rather hard to break down; you can "encourage" stubborn clays and shales by boiling the fossils slowly for about an hour. It will help if you add washing soda or a strong detergent to the water. But much of the excess rock and most of the softer material can be brushed away with a scrub brush or tooth brush. A small wire brush (similar to the type used to clean suede shoes) may be used to remove more stubborn rock fragments. Spread the fossils on newspaper and place them in the sun to dry. Or, if you wish, place them in a pan and dry them in the oven or over a radiator.

Mounted needles, tweezers, awls, and old dental tools are useful to clean more delicate fossils or around the smaller structures of larger specimens. You can make your own cleaning needle by setting the blunt end of a large needle in a five-inch long section of a ¼-inch dowel. It may be advisable to use a magnifying glass when working with small fossils or with delicate surface structures of larger specimens. If you mount the glass on a homemade stand, your hands will be left free to work with the fossil.

Excess pieces of hard rock can be trimmed away with hammer and cold chisel. *Caution* is the watchword here. This is an operation in which it is easy to harm the fossil or yourself. Always direct the chisel *away* from your hand, tap gently, and protect your eyes from flying rock chips. A slipping chisel or misplaced blow of the hammer can easily damage a fine fossil or tender finger!

Sometimes vinegar, which is weak acetic acid, will help clean fossils coated with limy rock such as limestone and shale. However, the beginner should, in general, avoid the use of stronger acids. These are not only apt to completely dissolve the fossil, they may cause property damage and inflict serious injury on the skin and eyes of the user.

Did one of your prize specimens get "fractured" on the way home? Or maybe the chisel slipped and split a fine fossil right down the middle!

Don't throw broken specimens away. Chances are they can be rather easily mended. Keep the fragments of the broken fossil together in the same tray. If you are good at puzzles you will soon have the broken parts properly fitted together. You can then clean the broken surfaces and apply strong household cement or glue to both pieces. Be sure to hold the parts tightly together until the glue has had time to make its initial set. Lay them aside to dry overnight and they will probably be almost as good as new.

Unfortunately, some fossils slowly crumble or otherwise deteriorate when they are exposed to the air. This can usually be remedied by giving the specimen a protective coating of pure white shellac, clear nail polish, or clear plastic spray. The latter comes in easy-to-use aerosol spray cans. Fragments of bone are particularly apt to crumble on exposure to the air. This type of fossil is normally quite fragile and should be excavated with great care and shellacked or sprayed as soon as dry.

Your fossils have been scrubbed up, patched up, and identified—now what? The next step is to make permanent labels for your specimens. Labels can be typed or written on good white paper or cards. On the label give the scientific name of the fossil, the geologic formation from which it was collected, exactly where it was found, the date and by whom it was collected. You can take this collecting data from the labels that were placed in each bag of fossils as they were collected, or from the field notebook.

This information should also be entered in some type of record book or on 3-by-5-inch filing cards. The cards should be given a number which corresponds to a number that is put on each fossil. This number, called a *catalog* or *specimen number*, should also appear on the label.

It you have a card catalog a sample card might look like this:

	Specimen No. K-162
NAME	Kingena Wacoensis
FORMATION	Duck Creek (Cret.)
LOCALITY	Cobb Park, Ft. Worth, Tex.
COLLECTOR	Jim Matthews
DATE 4/26/63	REMARKS *Good collecting spot; well preserved faund.*

On the other hand, if you decide to keep your records in a loose-leaf binder or composition book, you might enter each specimen as follows:

Catalog Number	Name	Formation	Locality	Collector	Date
32	Exogyra Texana	Goodland Formation	Lake Worth Ft. Worth, Tex.	Edward Williams	10-20-62

Illinois is one of the most renowned fossil sources in the world. Here are found fine plant fossils from the Pennsylvanian period.

Pennsylvanian outcrop area

The entries in the catalog should be numbered consecutively and each specimen should have its own individual catalog number. Some collectors also assign a *locality number* to all specimens from the same collecting locality. This is handy in looking up the collecting locality, but this number should not be confused with the catalog number.

The catalog number should be written with India ink on some inconspicuous place on the fossil. If the surface of the fossil is too coarse or porous for ink, place a small patch of quick-drying white enamel on the specimen. This is not always as easy as it sounds. The paint will sometimes run or streak and ruin a fine specimen. The wise thing to do is to practice on a piece of rock that you do not want before spotting the actual specimen. After the paint dries, the catalog number can be added in India ink. When the ink has dried, coat the number with a dab of clear shellac or clear nail polish. This will help preserve the number. What about those tiny fossils that are too small to write numbers on? Simply drop them into a small plastic or glass pill vial and write the number directly on the vial or on a piece of paper that can be placed inside.

You now have the same number on the fossil, the label, and in your catalog. If the specimen should become separated from its label, it can easily be identified by referring to the number you have placed on it.

Now that your fossils have been properly prepared and cataloged, the next step is to provide them with a good home. You will want to mount some of the better specimens to display in your room. However, lack of space may make it necessary to store some of them.

There are a number of ways in which you can take care of your fossil collection. But the way in which the specimens are stored or displayed will probably depend upon the amount of time, space, and money that you can allot to this phase of your hobby. Some collectors buy expensive cabinets and ready-made wooden or plastic trays. But thrift-minded rockhounds make their own fossil trays of cardboard and gummed tape—and have fun doing it.

After being placed in their trays, the fossils can then be displayed in an old china cabinet or bookcase, or on a whatnot shelf. Check your attic or basement—there may be pieces of old furniture just waiting to be put in your museum. If not, visit a store that sells used furniture. There you may find an old china cabinet with glass doors, this is ideal. Shine the glass, polish or paint the woodwork, and then place it in the den, family room, or your bedroom. You might even want to set up your museum in a storeroom or in a corner of your basement.

Specimens that are not on exhibit can be stored in shoe boxes, shirt boxes, or cigar boxes. These can easily be obtained from a neighborhood store. Coffee cans and jars can be used for this purpose. Cardboard egg cartons are also handy for storing fossils. The individual partitions are just the right size to hold a fossil and label. Partitions of cardboard can also be placed in shoe or cigar boxes. Or, if you prefer, you can buy heavy-duty display boxes with partitions already in them.

Match boxes make fine containers in which to keep small fossils. They stack neatly and several can be stored in a drawer or larger box. If you prefer an open display, remove the top of the matchbox and line the bottom with cotton. Place a fossil, and its accompanying label, neatly in the box and tape a clear cellophane cover on top. Presto, an attractive but very inexpensive display box! If you want to get fancy, paint the exterior of the box with watercolors or cover it with cloth or colored paper. Small pocket-sized showcases can be made in the same way from "penny" match boxes.

You can also use match boxes to make a small chest of drawers for storing fossils. To do this you will need the following:
1. Six large, empty match boxes of the same size.
2. Glue—one of the white glues which dries clear.
3. Covering material—cotton, rayon, construction paper, or "self-sticking" adhesive-backed plastic material.

Here is how it is made:
1. Remove each matchbox from its cover.
2. Cut a piece of covering material to fit the end of each matchbox. You will need 12 of these (about 1¼-by-1½ inches in size).
3. Glue one of these pieces to each end of the box.
4. When glue on the end-covers has dried, slip the box back into its cover.

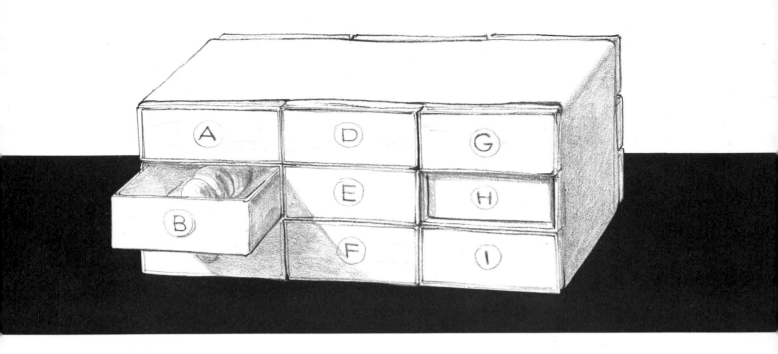

5. Next, join the matchboxes together. Glue two boxes side-by-side and then glue two more side-by-side on top of these. When all six boxes have been joined you will have three rows of two drawers each, or a total of six drawers.

6. Now, cut a strip of covering material wide enough to cover the boxes from front to back (roughly 4¾ inches) and long enough to go completely around the six mounted boxes. With a bit left to overlap, a strip about 20½ inches long will cover most chests.

7. Coat the back of the cover material with glue.

8. Place chest in center of the strip and glue the covering tightly around it. (It may be a good idea to make a "dry run" of this step before putting the glue on the cover.)

9. Drawer handles can be made of small fossils, shells, or brightly painted pieces of wood. Glue or sew these to the end of each box.

These attractive little chests will house a large number of smaller fossils. Best of all, they are fun to make.

Some collectors like to mount their fossils on small blocks of wood. If you bevel (or slant) the front of the block, you can attach a label to this part of it. To mount the fossil, place a bit of glue or household cement in the middle of the block and press the specimen firmly into it. Let it dry for a day or two before you move it.

Amphibians

Fishes

146   Invertebrates

You may have some delicate or unusual specimens you would like to show under glass. Such fossils can be safely displayed in a *Riker Mount*. This is a shallow, glass-topped, cardboard box that is filled with cotton. The specimen is placed on top of the cotton and is held in place by pressure exerted by the glass top against the specimen and cotton backing. The top of the mount is held in place by pins on each side of the box. You can make an attractive framed exhibit to hang on the wall if you apply adhesive picture hangers to the back of the mount. Riker Mounts come in a variety of sizes and can be obtained from most scientific supply houses.

If you like to make things, you can easily construct your own glass-topped display box. You will need a relatively shallow cardboard box (about 1½ inches is a good average depth). Cut an opening in the top

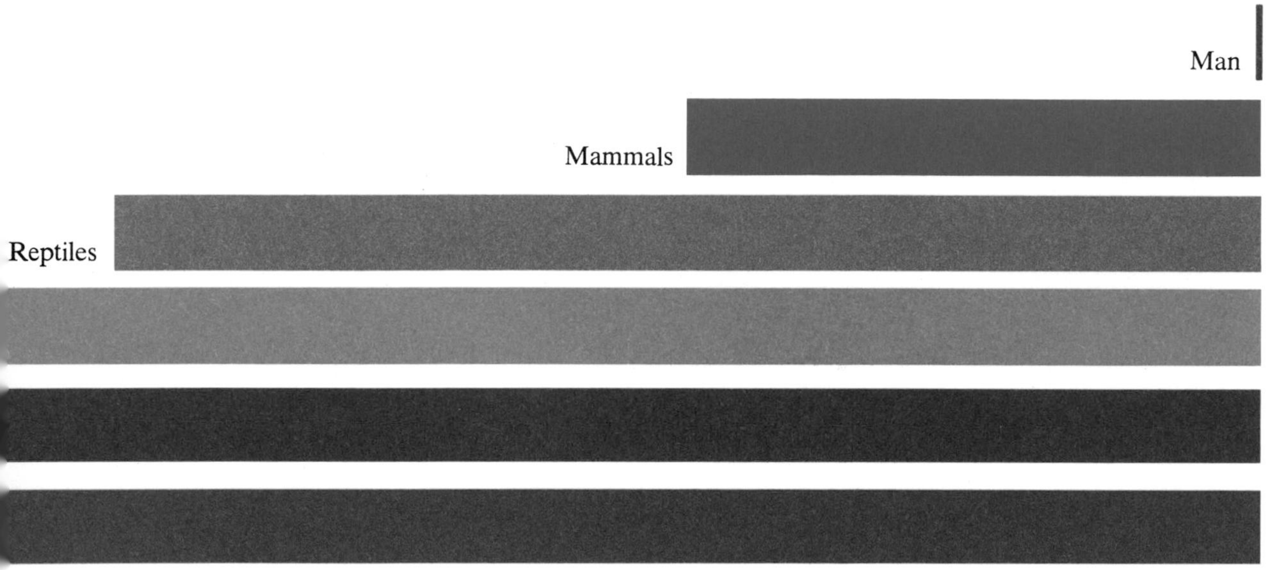

Man

Mammals

Reptiles

large enough to show the fossils you want to exhibit. Make the opening about one-half inch smaller than the glass. This will allow sufficient room to glue or tape the glass to the top. Thus, if you plan to use a standard 8-by-10-inch glass from a picture frame, cut an opening of no more than 7½ by 9½ inches. Of course, the top of your box would have to be at least 8-by-10 inches in size. Next, place a layer of clean cotton in the box. *Hint:* a nice flat layer can be peeled off a large roll of absorbent cotton. Now, carefully arrange the fossils on the cotton and place the glass-covered top on the box. Four pins, two on each side of the box, can be stuck through the sides to keep the top from coming off. You can cover the box or paint it if you wish.

To display larger fossils under glass, you may want to make a larger glass-topped exhibit case. Maybe you could build such a cabinet for your woodworking project in "shop."

One interesting way to mount fossils is on a display board. To put fossils on a board for museum display, glue them with one of the clear-drying, white glues. These glues are strong and may be used on wood, paper, cloth, and other porous material. Use plenty of glue and allow ample time for it to dry. Some specimens are too large and heavy to be cemented to the board. These can be attached by means of wire. Drill small holes through the display board on either side of where you want the fossil to be. Now, pass pieces of fine small wire over the fossil, through the holes, and twist the loose ends together at the back of the board.

A variety of material can be used to make display boards. Heavy cardboard, Upson board, masonite, plywood, and celotex are probably most commonly used. To hold the board erect and to keep it from warping, make a narrow wooden border around the edges. Screen molding is good for this purpose.

After the specimens have been wired or glued to the board, place a small white label beneath each specimen. On this, give the name and catalog number of the fossil. More information can be added if space will permit. In some instances you may be able to write directly on the board. However, the surface of most such boards will cause ink or paint to run.

Smaller specimens can be mounted on heavy pieces of white cardboard which have been ruled into squares. The name of the formation from which the fossils were collected can be written at the top of the card. Write the name and catalog number of each fossil in the square directly beneath the specimen. If you do not want to hang or stand the board up, cut the card to fit the bottom of a small cardboard carton or cigar box. Before filing them away, write the name of the formation on one end and on the top of the box. This will make them easier to locate after they have been stored.

Display boards can be used to make a variety of exhibits. Maybe you would like to mount all of the fossils collected from a certain geologic formation on the same board. Or, possibly you would like one board of brachiopods, another of corals, and still another showing only snails. There is no end to the variety of exhibits you can create.

Attractive exhibits can be made of fossils that have been partially embedded in plaster of Paris. In addition, some collectors have prepared interesting displays of fossils embedded in plastic.

Certain other types of displays can be shown with your fossils. Perhaps you would like to exhibit a map showing the areas in which the fossils were collected. Collecting localities can be designated by colored map pins or labels giving the locality number. A still better way is to mount the map above a table which contains representative fossils from each locality. Connect the fossils to their localities by means of ribbon or colored string. Or maybe you would prefer to mount the fossils and map on the same board.

Another interesting exhibit is one that shows the various ways in which fossils are formed. Use a board or a display case to show types of preservation as outlined in Chapter 4. For example, use a fish tooth or oyster shell for "Unaltered Hard Parts," carbonized leaf impression for "Carbonization," and petrified wood could be labeled "Petrifaction."

Some collectors make colorful wall posters showing the geologic time scale. The "Family Tree of Life" would make another interesting poster display.

These are but a few of the types of exhibits that might be placed in your earth history museum. Since most fossil collectors also collect rocks and minerals, these can be displayed along with your fossils. In fact, the same methods used in cleaning, labeling, and mounting fossils, can be used on most other geological specimens.

In arranging your exhibits remember that they should be attractive, educational, and interesting. The best displays are those that tell a story that will stimulate the mind and interest of the viewer. The specimens should be as clean as possible and correctly and clearly labeled. They should be arranged in an attractive, orderly, and uncrowded manner.

Needless to say, your earth science museum could be the basis for an excellent project in your science class or for a science fair. You may even wish to enter your exhibit at a rock and mineral club convention or the county fair.

Where to look for fossils

For those
who want to
know more

The publications listed below have been especially selected for the reader who wishes to explore further the wonderful world of fossils.

Andrews, Roy C. *All About Dinosaurs*. Random House, New York, 1953.

Casanova, Richard. *An Illustrated Guide to Fossil Collecting*. Naturegraph Publishing Co., Healdsburg, California, 1957.

Colbert, Edwin H. *The Dinosaur Book*. McGraw-Hill, New York, 1951.

Farb, Peter. *The Story of Life: Plants and Animals Through the Ages*. Harvey House, Inc., Irvington-on-Hudson, New York, 1962.

Fenton, Carroll L. and Fenton, Mildred A. *The Fossil Book*. Doubleday, New York, 1958.

Fox, William and Welles, Samuel. *From Bones to Bodies: A Story of Paleontology*. Henry Z. Walck, Inc., New York, 1959.

Ludovici, L. J. *The Great Tree of Life, Paleontology: The Natural History of Living Creatures*. Putnam, New York, 1963.

Matthews, William H., III. *Fossils: An Introduction to Prehistoric Life*. Barnes and Noble, New York, 1962.

Matthews, William H., III. *Texas Fossils*. Bureau of Economic Geology, University of Texas, Austin, Texas, 1960.

Matthews, William H., III. *Wonders of the Dinosaur World*. Dodd, Mead, New York, 1963.

Petersen, Kai. *Prehistoric Life on Earth*. E. P. Dutton & Co., New York, 1961.

Reed, W. Maxwell. *The Earth for Sam* (Revised edition by Paul Brandwein). Harcourt, Brace and World, Inc., New York, 1960.

Rhodes, Frank H. T.; Zim, Herbert S.; and Shaffer, Paul R. *Fossils: A Guide to Prehistoric Life*. Golden Press, New York, 1963.

Scheele, William E. *Prehistoric Animals*. World Publishing Company, Cleveland, Ohio, 1954.

153

Photograph on title page from Geology Department, Lamar State College of Technology, Beaumont, Texas.

INDEX

154

155

157